WE ARE ALL MIGRANTS

WE ARE ALL MIGRANTS

Political Action and the Ubiquitous Condition of Migrant-hood

GREGORY FELDMAN

stanford briefs
An Imprint of Stanford University Press
Stanford, California

Stanford University Press
Stanford, California

Printed in the United States of America
on acid-free, archival-quality paper

Library of Congress Cataloging-in-Publication Data

Feldman, Gregory, 1969– author.
  We are all migrants : political action and the ubiquitous condition of
migrant-hood / Gregory Feldman.
    pages cm
  Includes bibliographical references.
  ISBN 978-0-8047-8933-2 (pbk. : alk. paper)
  1. Political alienation. 2. Political participation. 3. Political psychology.
4. Power (Social sciences) 5. Political science—Philosophy. I. Title.
  JA74.5.F47 2015
  323.3'2912—dc23

                                                            2015004651

ISBN 978-0-8047-9588-3 (electronic)

Typeset by Classic Typography in 10/13 Adobe Garamond

FOR ARMANDO,
WHO MADE ME REALIZE THAT FREEDOM
BEGINS WITH THINKING.

FOR TY,
WITH WHOM I WANDERED THROUGH THE
HILLS OF BOXGROVE, ENGLAND, AND
WONDERED WHAT LIFE MIGHT HAVE BEEN
LIKE IN THE LOWER PALEOLITHIC.

I know somewhat too much; and from this knowledge, once one has been infected, there seems to be no recovering. I ought never to have taken my lantern to see what was going on in the hut by the granary. On the other hand, there was no way, once I had picked up the lantern, for me to put it down again.

—J. M. Coetzee, *Waiting for the Barbarians*

CONTENTS

PREFACE

Archaeologists estimate that at least a hundred thousand years ago
anatomically modern humans began migrating out of what we
now call Africa. They traveled through today's Sinai Peninsula and
Horn of Africa, into the Middle East, and then throughout the
Eurasian landmass. Their journeys would have involved the pursuit
of game, pressures from rival bands, climatic and environmental
changes, or a combination thereof. If these journeys transpired
over centuries or millennia, then perhaps they would not have even
recognized them as migrations. We can reasonably assume that
each generation encountered only slight shifts in location rather
than an epic trek "out of Africa," as we might see it today. If significant parts of the journey transpired over a few generations, then it
could have played a central role in collective memory. A sense of
estrangement might have characterized the lore that was narrated
to children. These people might have felt nostalgia for lost kin and
for the familiar landscapes they once effortlessly navigated. The old
deities, dwelling in the grasses, trees, and shrubs, who could help
or hinder the daily goings-on, would have become the stuff of leg-
ends, and new ones would have been encountered. The new game
they hunted might have ranged in less predictable circuits. Rather
than ally with neighboring clans that were easily located in their

cosmologies, they would now have negotiated naïvely with strangers, or perhaps, gone to war with them. This sense of loss would suggest that these migrating hominids did not simply live *in* places faraway from where they now stood, but were *of* those places, which they themselves made. Through worldly artifices of their own making, they directly manipulated resources and imbued the surrounding landscape with meaning so as to render the strange familiar. Yet while the worlds they left now lay beyond the horizon, it is equally reasonable to assume that these hominids constituted new worlds as they and their descendants moved in new directions. Thus, while people in the prehistoric world likely experienced broken connections to people and place, alienation was not the sine qua non of daily life. The reason was certainly not that the worlds they built lasted forever after they moved on. Rather, they built for themselves the worlds they inhabited, even as they moved from place to place. In other words, to inhabit a place is to directly constitute it as such with others. Absent systemic alienation from persons and place, these hominids cannot be referred to as *migrants* even though we describe their journey "out of Africa" as a *migration*.

In contrast to the prehistoric case of migrations without migrants, modernity presents us with an opposing situation: migrants without migrations. While most contemporary migration involves movement, we would be deceived to think that movement is the migrant's definitive quality. The case of ethnic Russians born in Estonia and Latvia during the Soviet era illustrates the point's central importance. By 1991, the Estonian and Latvian movements for political autonomy within the Soviet Union ended up fully restoring the independence of the pre-Soviet republics. These movements' leadership did not declare independence for the first time because each country had already been a sovereign nation-state with membership in the League of Nations. That (re)independence leaders could legitimately hold this position depended upon their ability to legally demonstrate what was already common knowledge: neither country had willfully joined the USSR in 1940. They found their evidence in the secret protocols of the 1939 Molotov-Ribbentrop Pact named for the Soviet and German foreign ministers who negotiated the agreement. With the pact, Stalin agreed to leave western Poland in Hitler's sphere of influence in exchange for Hitler leaving to Stalin eastern Poland, Lithuania, Latvia, Estonia, and Finland. Shortly after its signing, Stalin forced Estonia, Latvia, and Lithuania into joining the Soviet Union. Neither Winston Churchill nor Franklin Roosevelt recognized the Baltic republics as constituent members of the Soviet Union, but rather denounced the accession as an illegitimate and forced annexation. Many other Western governments followed suit. Hence, Estonian and Latvian (and also Lithuanian) leaders in the late 1980s could argue on internationally accepted legal and political grounds that they were restoring, rather than establishing, national sovereignty. This crucial distinction enabled the democratically elected leadership of these restored nation-states to control citizenship policy as it occurs in any other sovereign state. Estonia and Latvia restored their pre-Soviet nationality laws, thus restoring citizenship to anyone who had held it prior to the 1940 Soviet annexation and to anyone who descended from such a citizen, according to jus sanguinis (right of blood). This law included a modest number of ethnic Russians and their descendants who lived in these countries prior to World War II. At the same time, it produced migrants out of well over a million people, mostly ethnic Russians, who either arrived soon after World War II to rebuild their lives or were simply born in these republics. Denied citizenship in the restored republics, they were immediately rendered stateless. They could acquire citizenship only through EU-accepted naturalization procedures, which included passing national language and civics exams and accumulating the necessary years of legal residence in the sovereign post-Soviet republics. (Their years accumulated during the Soviet era did not count because the Soviet Union illegally held Estonian and Latvian national sovereignty in abeyance.) This outcome, given its consistency with the logic of state sovereignty, satisfied the Western diplomatic community. From the perspective of the new stateless, however, they had never crossed an international border when moving to Estonia or Latvia, because they had remained within the Soviet Union. They did not regard themselves as migrants. They had established their roots and had no place to which they could return in the new Russian Federation, even if they wished. Russia was not their home. They became migrants without migrations because the Soviet border literally swept eastward under their feet with the reestablishment of Estonian and Latvian independence. They had not moved an inch when their world was reconstituted for them.

To compare migrations without migrants to migrants without migrations is to raise an urgent question. What is it, precisely, that has moved when someone in today's world is called a migrant? Is it simply the person who steps over an international border with or without official travel documents? I will argue not only that this peculiar act is not what distinguishes the migrant and the citizen, but that these two characters are fundamentally indistinguishable. What renders people "migrants" is their lack of possibility to constitute (and reconstitute) the places they inhabit in direct negotiation with others inhabiting those same places. This unfortunate condition—the condition of *migrant-hood*—detaches people from each other, rendering them migrants, unmoored in a shifting sea of other migrants. Migrant-hood does not capture the experience of the migrating hunter-gatherer band, yet it fundamentally conditions the lives of both the modern "citizen" and the "migrant." It would not be accurate to assert that "we are all citizens" if that status is supposed to embody the quintessence of modern political empowerment. Even citizens of liberal democracies, to say nothing of the migrants in them, feel far removed from the mass party politics that govern their national societies. The term "global citizen" (an oxymoron) seems more like a cynical joke to keep people traveling in worldwide labor circuits or venturing abroad to consume cultural experiences, a vital part of the global economy. By default, we are all migrants.

We must look beyond the legal differences between a citizen and a migrant so that we may understand how, contrary to expectations, the lives of both are similarly conditioned. Both are subject to the ebbs and flows of their labor markets; both experience separations from family and friends; both can find their familiar surroundings strangely unfamiliar when development marches rampantly onward; both lack substantial control over the technocratic decisions that condition their lives; and both may find that reaching out for help from someone within arm's length feels like a futile stretch across a canyon. Can we not therefore remove the veil of citizenship to get a clearer view of who the migrant really is? The point of this exercise is not to foolishly claim that migrants would receive more respect if only they were treated like citizens. Rather, it is to argue that the sense of protection and permanence that citizenship seems to offer can deaden the citizen's own sensitivity to the political disempowerment of which the migrant is more likely to be aware.

This book aims to bridge the gap between the academy and the broader public. However, it strives to do this without watering down the intellectual content, which would render it useless for the academic's pursuit of knowledge, and condescending to the interested reader within a wider audience. To avoid this pitfall, the book must ask readers in either camp to modify, but not minimize, their expectations. To the academic reader, it asks that we not recognize knowledge production solely as the result of the expert pushing ever further into unchartered corners of specialization. The limits of this singular conception of knowledge production are flagged by the remarkably short shelf life of the vast majority of the products of our labor (journal articles, monographs, and increasingly video documentaries). This book takes a different tack. It is not a piece of specialized research, but rather an effort to redeploy existing, critical concepts in new ways for the sake of better understanding migrant-hood and political action in the present world. This project is analogous to the paleontologist who seeks new discoveries not mainly through field excavations, but also by considering how known fossils sitting on the laboratory shelves could be reassembled to reveal an unidentified species. Knowledge can be produced on either path.

To any other reader, I hope that the argument shows the merit of a different perspective on migration, citizenship, and political action, one that is not commonly expressed but is directly relevant. Despite not being a standard research monograph, the book still asks that the reader neither assume a mainstream perspective nor dismiss unfamiliar concepts as academic elitism. If concepts used in this argument are unintelligible, then the problem lies either with the limits of my own powers of explanation or with readers' reluctance to leave their comfort zones. To keep up my end of the bargain, I have tried to avoid technical jargon, which is merely shorthand that, if used well, allows experts to carry out their own internal discussions more efficiently. This is especially the case when one concept presupposes another. (Imagine if physicists had to reiterate Newton's *Principia Mathematica* every time they wished to discuss motion.) Any interested individual can follow the train of thought if the shorthand is elaborated in shared language. I can think of no better public role for the academic than one that articulates counterintuitive perspectives on the world "out there" of which others may be intuitively aware but lack the time or opportunity to fully explore and discuss with others. To be sure, political action requires first a clear formulation of that which oppresses us and how it does so. Our capacity to understand these matters can only help us devise new ways to rectify what we agree to be injustices.

ACKNOWLEDGMENTS

I would like to thank several people for the help and support they provided as I wrote the manuscript. Jenna Dixon, Melissa Gregg, Nick Palaj, Ogake Angwenyi, and Sara Sim conducted research assistance at different moments through the process. John Harriss and Alec Dawson carved out space for me at Simon Fraser University's School for International Studies, thereby offering vital material support. Discussions with Samir Gandesha helped clarify certain parts of the argument. I am grateful to Sandro Mezzadra and Manuela Bojadzijev for inviting me to the summer school "Expanding the Margins: Migrations, Mobilities, Borders" at the Institute for European Ethnology at Humboldt University, Berlin, in September 2014. I presented a version of this argument there and benefited from the questions and comments from participants—in particular, Ralph Litzinger and Stephen Scheel. I am grateful for Michelle Lipinski's reliable and constructive editorial input throughout this book's production. Jeff Wyneken's copy-editing no doubt improved the flow of the text. I thank Merje Kuus for crucial support at home.

WE ARE ALL MIGRANTS

INTRODUCTION

The Presence of Migrant-hood and the Absence of Politics

To argue that we are all migrants is not to partake in an act of liberal patronage. It has become fashionable to seek political or moral capital by expressing a shared identity with collectivized groups in less fortunate circumstances. The specific contents of that identity remain strategically vague, often invoking descriptors such as "human" or entities such as "humanity," whatever these terms may mean. These proclamations of togetherness may succeed in shipping a few resources from the affluent to the needy. But here is the rub. Whoever proclaims such a universal identity is, in effect, speaking *for* others rather than *with* another. The speaker is not engaging the other in a dialogue of equals, because the other is not empowered to switch the sentence's subject (the speaker) and its direct object (the one spoken for, the "other"). Subjects may speak; objects cannot. The social structure and the grammatical structure work together.

A case in point is found in a media campaign by the "Keep a Child Alive" charity. It consisted of posters featuring Western celebrities in what appears as decorative African face paint as a show of solidarity with African children suffering from AIDS. The large script caption at the bottom of the posters reads, "I am African." Sting, David Bowie, Liv Tyler, Gwyneth Paltrow, Sarah Jessica

1

Parker, and Elijah Wood among others offered their images in support of this cause. The campaign's premise maintained that since all people must ultimately trace their ancestry to prehistoric people who migrated out of Africa, the ethical course of action is to enhance the quality of life of African children because we share a common origin. In the words of the campaign itself:

> As we live our lives in the West, perhaps we forget our origins. It is well know [sic] that each of us originated in Africa from our African ancestors. Indeed it was these incredible people who traveled far and wide and whose genes are in all of us. . . . Indeed, if we let Africa die then we are letting the origins of our species perish.[1]

Not all Africans, however, share this sense of common humanity, but rather interpret it as more liberal patronage from those would enhance their profile against the suffering of children living in Africa. One counterimage modeled on the campaign motif that circulated online featured an African woman in traditional dress with the caption, "I am Gwyneth Paltrow." A scathing indictment of celebrity activism and faux solidarity appeared in small print at the bottom of the poster[2]:

> I am Gwyneth Paltrow: help us stop the shameless famewhores from using the suffering of those dying from AIDS in Africa to bolster their pathetic careers now that they are no longer dating Brad Pitt and no one gives a shit about them. Just kiss my Black ass to help.

To my knowledge, no major funding from Western sources resulted from this plea. It can be a bit uncomfortable when the "other" speaks. The rage expressed in the counterimage's caption reveals the frustration of being spoken *for*, when one is not empowered to speak as an equal about how we should live together in this

---

1. http://keepachildalive.org/media/campaigns/i-am-african/; accessed March 12, 2014.

2. http://thisisnotafrica.tumblr.com/post/28001392173/text-in-picture -reads-i-am-gwyneth-paltrow-help; accessed March 12, 2014.

world. The original campaign's invocation of a common humanity functions as a device to silence particular voices, which might question the world order, rather than as an invitation to negotiate its order.

The assertion of a common humanity that drowns out particular speaking subjects can be found anywhere. In a far more innocuous example, in my hometown of Vancouver, city buses project larger-than-life images of professional hockey players screaming victoriously in their full game regalia before legions of fans. The banner headline running across the side of the bus declares, "We are all Canucks." I do not personally know these hockey players, and I cannot identify any particular fan in the arena. The image gives no indication of what a Canuck actually is or why I should be one. Yet it speaks for me and demands that I, and any particular individual across the city, melt into an essentialized municipal whole in which we are all one and so none of us is anyone in particular. If this view seems to make a mountain out of a molehill, then consider a reverse equation similar to the "I am Gwyneth Paltrow" counterimage mocking the "Keep a Child Alive" campaign. Most certainly, TransLink (Metro Vancouver's public transit operator) would hardly be interested in plastering my image across a city bus underneath the headline, "We are all Greg Feldman." Such a headline would instantly spotlight an absurdity: while a mass of particular individuals can be dissolved into a *generic* figure, that mass cannot be reduced to any *particular* individual because no two particular individuals are identical. Yet the fact that we need satire to highlight this point reveals the banality of our belief in common human essences, which are expressed in abstract singular figures like "Canuck" or "African" or, in parody, "Stephen Colbert," leader of the mock Colbert Nation.

This belief comes at a cost. Unexpectedly, the woman in Africa, posing ironically as Gwyneth Paltrow, and yours truly hold something in common that we share with countless others: fundamentally, we do not matter politically, because we cannot speak as particular people. We can only be spoken for, once we are lumped into mass, stereotyped groups (for example, voters between ages 18 and 30; refugees; consumers earning more than $400,000 per year; radicals; fellow citizens; the working poor; job applicants with a master's degree; immigrants admitted on a three-month work permit; and so on). I am not suggesting that those who cannot speak are all essentially the same or that their different positions in the global socioeconomic hierarchy do not matter. Rather, I argue that people qua particular individuals share a common condition of *atomization* (and not a common essence) that renders our particular, individual differences politically inconsequential, or at least creates a situation in which our particularity can only politically appear *despite* the "system," not *because* of it. Wealthy individuals are obviously better positioned to reproduce structures of inequality to their own advantage, but this is something different (and still unacceptable) from political empowerment.

This book argues that we are all migrants because in today's world people face common conditions of existence for a life experience proverbially understood as that of a "migrant": rootless, uncertain, atomized, disempowered. If so, then it stands to reason that the root causes of the hardships that migrants face degrade the lives of citizens as well, potentially if not actually. This position does not trivialize the hardship confronting migrants, particularly from the Global South, or claim that a middle-class Northern citizen viscerally understands the loss of a child on a clandestine journey across a sea or desert. Instead, it argues that the basic conditions that make it reasonable to risk such a journey underpin contemporary politics, economy, and society across the globe and so affect, if to a different degree, the life chances of the proverbial middle-class Northern citizen. If that citizen has not faced the same dilemma as that migrant, then the difference is explained by their respective locations in a global socioeconomic hierarchy that, likewise, can turn against the citizen in the right historical moment. To elaborate, Jean and John Comaroff argue that the violence plaguing the transitions to liberal democracy in the postcolonies is not antithetical to a tranquil North more experienced in peace and democracy. Rather, it is only a more robust manifestation of similar Northern problems resulting from such Northern-led initiatives as neoliberalism, state disintegration, and the substitution of policing for politics. The postcolonies more fully express the conditions in which "we" live in the North; "their" world is "ours" too. Hence, people in either place might have reason to see each other as partners in political action.

In the formulation "we are all migrants" I locate the impetus to political action in the existential question, "Do I, in particular, matter in this world?" a question prompted by the condition of migrant-hood itself. Readers with leftist orientations might find this approach uncompelling, preferring instead to begin with the structures of inequality that generate conflict and struggles between opposing actors. They might consign existential angst to one's private life in order to get on to the public matters of socioeconomic inequality. I think that these two orientations to political action do not conflict because the existential question itself only becomes possible through modern alienation, which is deeply intertwined with socioeconomic factors. Readers with a liberal-humanitarian perspective might find the focus on one's existential angst to be overly self-absorbed and thus insufficiently attuned to the suffering of others in worse circumstances. However, such angst does not spontaneously sprout from one's psychological constitution, but rather it emerges through one's attempt to negotiate surrounding social, economic, and political conditions facing both migrants and citizens. Armed with the insight that our deepest anxieties are composed in the same historical field of human relations, then "their" struggles no longer seem so foreign to "mine." They might even begin to look similar.

The importance of honoring the existential question as the impetus to action is that it hits us with urgency and immediacy and in such a way that cannot be fully explained to anyone else. We must seek explanations for it after we acknowledge its presence. Does this angst come from a psychological disposition? from a medical condition? from social relationships? from economic exploitation? from cultural changes? In any case, the theoretical explanation we choose only provides us with understanding; by itself, theoretical reason does not instigate action. Instead, the angst's very immanence deep in our interior selves—that unquestionably subjective experience—compels us to ask not only "why" but also "what can I do?" From this vantage point, that angst-ridden question will only be satisfied in the world "out there" with others, when people mutually constitute themselves as particular speaking subjects in what Hannah Arendt called *spaces of appearance*.

Spaces of appearance arise when people organize themselves to ask if the world they live in is the world they want to inhabit, and if not, what could be done differently. It makes no difference whether the specific issues they address are large or small, or of global or local consequence. Either way, spaces of appearance are the embodiment of political action among particular speaking subjects. The reason why someone would want to constitute such a space is not necessarily to gain access to vital resources (and often this is not the core problem). Access to resources keeps our bodies alive, but it does not address the existential question, which reverses the biological question's priorities: rather than ask, "How can I survive?" it asks what the point of keeping my body alive is if nothing more matters. This existential question, of course, does not deny the primary need to survive, but instead aims at the will to live through one's particular life as fully as possible. It therefore speaks to the power of natality (the fact that "I" in particular was born, though I might not have been) more than the power of fatality (the fact that "I," like all others, will inevitably die). From this distinction, the question follows that if I was not born into this particular life, and do not experience it as a conscious individual, then what meaningful difference does it make if that fateful day comes sooner rather than later?

The existential question is ultimately a political question because the will to appear means much more than simply being appreciated by others. The will to appear reveals a drive to play a constitutive role in the world, which we invariably share with others. It begins with dissatisfaction with how the individual herself allows injustice to perpetuate in the world by passively reproducing that world through her own daily routines. The apparent helplessness to help signifies more than a frustrated wish to "do good." Rather, it signifies the drive to act in the world under one's own volition. This motivation does not imply altruism, but neither does it imply pure self-interest. Instead, the unjust situation generates the existential question because she has determined that her ethical conflict with the world has become so great that she (1) cannot appear in it as her own particular self; and (2) cannot live with herself as agent of that injustice, even if she only plays a passive role in its perpetuation. If her perspective creates no impact through a worldly appearance, then the sad conclusion is that she in particular does not matter, and angst continues. Her particular *self* has no worldly presence; it cannot be confirmed by any other person; and so she is frustrated, atomized, and voiceless for lack of anyone else with whom to speak about that conflict. The sheer agony of this silencing effect was simply but brilliantly portrayed in Munch's famous painting "The Scream," which has been so successfully reduced to a cliché that its political insight is now all but lost.

The existential struggle to reach agreement with herself about how to conduct herself in that unjust world begins with thinking. Thinking is the two-in-one dialogue between her and herself that she undertakes in order to understand an ethical dilemma from the perspectives of others involved. Specifically, thinking is a discussion within an individual naturally divided into two equal parts (myself and I) aimed at unifying one's particular self. The unified self, however, only obtains a worldly reality if others recognize it in speech or action. The end of her condition of migranthood begins if she finds others willing to seriously consider the ethical viewpoint that emerged from her thinking and the action that it implies. As thinking individuals gather as particular speaking subjects, they constitute spaces of appearance that exist only as long as they jointly undertake the actions they deem necessary to deliberate and rectify the injustice. Their particularity of perspectives enables them to judge ethical dilemmas that do not fall into the rubric of pregiven laws, customs, and habits. In other words, when just action cannot be deduced from an established principle, then they must decide for the first time how justice can be achieved in such a way that allows them to maintain inner agreement in their dialogues of thought. The creation of this space, however, requires more than just *thinking* and *judging*. It also requires *willing*, the impulse to act in the world. Like the faculty of thinking, the will is also divided against itself because every volition the individual has to act is internally confronted by an opposite force to refrain from action: she wills, but she also wills not. When she resolves the conflict between her two wills, then she is poised to constitute a public space with others who have done the same. The space of appearance is a function of the joint action itself. It does not matter that people will not share the exact same opinion, but only that they can reach agreement on a course of action. These spaces are as varied as the countless possibilities of human assembly, yet all share the common purpose of doing justice to the cause of the angst in each person.

Without such spaces of appearance, the thinking individual—seeking to reach agreement with herself—receives no affirmation of her particular personhood and cannot appear in the world even if her will would so command her. She remains suspended eternally in a dialogue with herself, separated from the empirical world, and unable to satisfy her will to appear in concert with others. The obvious psychological problems that result from this miserable situation are thus rooted in the state that surrounds her (that is, the status quo) rather than in the state of her mental health. These problems are primarily political, not psychological. The will to appear is intrinsically a political act necessary to evade atomization and loneliness. Furthermore, once spaces of appearance dissipate, those who constituted them return to the atomized condition of migrant-hood if they have no home to which they can temporarily retreat. Atomization is not a situation in which people cannot cooperate due to physical separation. Atomized people cooperate all the time, particularly at work. Instead, it is a condition in which the unique perspective that each individual inherently possesses—simply because no two people have lived the same life—cannot be brought to bear on the question, "Why are we, as people living together, doing things in one way and not another?" If people are poised to ask this question, then people as particular speaking subjects would constitute their own sovereign spaces as they negotiated the given issue and acted accordingly. Spaces of appearance show politics as a positive endeavor reified by acts of constitution and reconstitution by particular speaking subjects. By positive, I surely do not mean morally correct in absolutist terms. Spaces of appearance are not utopias; no such thing exists, of course. These spaces are positive in the sense that "I," and the others in them, obtain a worldly existence as "myself" at my best, that is, actualized as the particular person I am. We must understand politics as such an act if the term is to gain a dignified meaning.

Our contemporary view of politics is largely negative, signified as gratuitous self-interest, or as something that has to be done so that economic activity can smoothly proceed, or as necessary acts that break down injustices better than they build new things in their place. To be sure, organized resistance often assembles in spaces of appearance so that the negative act of resistance against large-scale structures can transpire through the positive assembly of a public composed of particular speaking subjects. This experience can appeal to anyone alienated in mass society regardless of their particular political views. Hence, in contrast to the default view of politics as something negative, this book argues that in its positive form politics brings us to life as particular individuals, because to the existential question of whether "I" in particular matter, it answers, "Yes, because this place could not *be* what it is without me, just as I cannot *be* without this place." These moments are the instantiations of freedom.

But why are we all migrants rather than workers, family members, inhabitants of the earth, or some other category? Why focus on migrant-hood as a defining status of modern life rather than something else? The reason for focusing on migrant-hood is to clarify the relationship between two contemporary phenomena that we do not usually associate with each other. The first is a worldwide obsession with migration. People tend to have firm views about it. The figure of "the migrant" plays a prominent role in the collective imagination and in national politics, testifying that nationalism remains deeply entrenched in personal identities as well. The migrant's presence on this front is curious since migrants amount to only three percent of the world's population according to United Nations estimates. On a global scale, migrants do not reach extraordinarily large numbers, unlike work-ers, women, or postcolonial subjects. However, the "migrant" now dominates public debate more than any other categorical subject. This character usually appears as a stereotyped threat to national purity; as an economic resource that fills holes in the labor mar-ket; or as a victim of tragedy that must be saved and quickly returned home. Yet in insisting that the migrant is fundamentally different from the citizen (that is, that "they" are different from "us"), we obscure the shared conditions that undermine our polit-ical agency as well as theirs.

The second phenomenon is a growing sense of disenfranchise-ment with mass party politics in representative democracies. While the liberal democratic tradition has succeeded right up to the pres-ent in liberating people from tyranny, dictatorship, and autocracy, it has arguably exhausted itself as far as incorporating people as political equals into decision-making processes that affect basic conditions of their daily lives. We are asked to respond to initiatives far more than to partake in acts of political constitution itself. The ballot box has become little more than a suggestion box; money and media hype make a mockery of the jingle, "Your voice counts." Hence, activist groups around the world, regardless of their goals or political orientations, seem to hold in common the drive to establish methods, often found in their own organizational forms, through which direct democracy can transpire on the basis of their own lived experiences. Examples of such groups range from those confusingly described as anarchist or antiglobalist to those more familiar to the mainstream, such as church groups, community organizations, and internet activists. They make clear that people from around the world dearly want political presence, and not just (if it all) a more comfortable Northern, middle-class lifestyle, a prospect that is vanishing along with the Northern middle-class itself. Curiously, they want it in a time when liberal democracy is by far the most dominant of modern ideologies; it triumphed over communism twenty-five years ago and those two together defeated fascism forty-five years earlier.

Bringing these two points together, this book maintains that (1) modernity as we know it creates the conditions for permanent migrant-hood threatening to atomize everyone it touches, citizen and migrant alike; (2) this pervasive condition of migrant-hood undermines joint political action, leaving people isolated, frustrated, and lonely; and (3) conversely, where joint political action appears, migrant-hood dissipates. The acquisition of national citizenship is not the bridge between the "migrant" and the "citizen," because something much more fundamental underpins both their possibilities of existence, namely, the obstacles they confront when trying to constitute themselves so that they can directly negotiate the basis of their coexistence with others.

Giorgio Agamben picks up on the link between migrant-hood and the absence of one's political selfhood when discussing Arendt's chapter "The Decline of the Nation-State and the End of the Rights of Man" in *The Origins of Totalitarianism*. Arendt highlights the central position of the migrant to explain the absence of political rights within the nation-state system. In that discussion, the migrant, signified as the stateless refugee, falls outside of state protection entirely. She points out that the very figure who most urgently tested the liberal system of universal rights was instead systematically denied them in interwar Europe. It is well known that Agamben argues from here that each individual citizen of the modern state is a potential refugee insofar as she becomes devoid of basic rights and political voice when the sovereign declares a security crisis (the "state of exception"). Law is suspended at that moment and the sovereign may act with impunity to reestablish the state's equilibrium as it sees fit. Those against whom the sovereign acts are *homo sacer* ("sacred man," that is, a voiceless, abstract person who is pushed outside of mundane, legal order). The slippery slope to the status of *homo sacer*—from citizen to refugee, that is—rests on the citizen's blurry, inside/outside position with respect to the nation-state. Though not formulated in precisely the following terms (or in terms of labor at all), Agamben argues that the citizenry's ambiguous position requires, on the one hand, their *presence* as atomized, abstract bodies on whom national sovereignty is imposed and from whom labor power is extracted; that is, as generic national citizens and exchangeable abstract laborers. On the other, it demands their *absence* as particular speaking subjects lest people qua particular individuals directly constitute their own sovereign spaces in spite of the nation-state and recognize their laboring activities as something that only keeps them alive, biologically speaking, but does not, by itself, beget their freedom. Hence, citizens are both inside and outside the sovereign nation-state. The state depends on them while simultaneously neglecting their particular political perspectives, just as the global economy depends on their labor but is ready to dismiss particular laborers at the first convenience. The citizen-laborer's structural position is not categorically different from that of the migrant legally understood. The laws that differentiate them ultimately stand on mushy ground. These countless silenced individuals, capable of acting as particular speaking subjects by virtue of their plurality, which Arendt recognized as a basic human condition, are akin to how Hardt and Negri later described the "multitude," which lives as Empire's creative underbelly, a vital force that apparatuses of rule must constantly appropriate in order to nullify its political potency.

I approach this argument largely through comparison. Ethnography and comparison are the twin pillars of anthropological method, although the latter is now much less appreciated than the former. Comparison in this book is not between two discrete, contemporary societies. (There is no such thing as a discrete society in any case). It is between historically produced tenets of social, economic, and political life that have appeared at different points in time and place. The purpose of comparison is not to suggest that a Golden Age once existed somewhere else that we should try to recover. It is not a project of nostalgia. Instead, the point is to use a radically different perspective on politics and selfhood to highlight the contours of our own contemporary experience in these realms. Such comparisons expose the limits of our experience so that we can begin to think past that which pushes us into the condition of migrant-hood by thinking past the migrant-citizen divide. The comparisons used in this argument often go beyond differences between "subject positions" within social formations, such as the difference between rich and poor in capitalist society or colonized and colonizer in imperial society. The reason is surely not indifference to those in weaker power positions. Rather, it is to caution that even the luxury of being in a stronger power position does not entail political empowerment in the positive sense of the term. As such, the wealthy and the powerful are no less atomized and no less denied a space of appearance than the poor and the weak. Access to resources allows the powerful to reproduce structural inequalities in their favor while declaring their priorities for the sake of the collective good. However, this is not politics understood positively. To paraphrase Giuseppe di Lampedusa, the aristocratic Italian author, it is merely private individuals justifying private interests by means of vague public ideals.

To do this comparative work, this book uses primarily "core" texts but also some current events. The texts range from Homer's *Iliad* and *Odyssey* to Coetzee's *Waiting for the Barbarians*, and from Tocqueville to Levi, Foucault, and Agamben. Readers familiar with Hannah Arendt's work will notice the particular influence of *The Human Condition*, *Lectures on Kant's Political Philosophy*, and *The Life of the Mind*. *The Human Condition* (which receives far more attention than the other two posthumously published books) has been criticized as nostalgia for the Greek polis and as an argument for liberal politics. These misleading conclusions, I maintain, result from a limited view of her full oeuvre and neglect her creative use of varying strands of thought. Arendt reaches her trenchant critique of modern political apathy (in which she includes instrumental liberalism in particular) through a contrast with the ancient world, not a celebration of it. Likewise, my opening comparison to the hunter-gatherer bands migrating "out of Africa" is not a romantic view of prehistoric life unadulterated by modern civilization. Instead, it offers a radical comparison with other forms of life, now long dead, in order to expose what we have difficulty understanding about the absence of politics in the present moment. Similarly, when explaining the importance of studying Lenin, Slavoj Žižek captures the methodological point that "the idea is not to return to Lenin but to repeat him in the Kierkegaardian sense: to retrieve the same impulse in today's constellation." Studying Lenin, then, does not mean to slavishly repeat what Lenin did, but to recover the possibilities that he opened up, even if his particular solution, in Žižek's words, "failed monstrously."

Finally, the argument may appear reductionist. My approach is not meant to deny the complexities and countervailing tendencies fully present in the world. On the contrary, it is to clarify as fully as possible how the condition of migrant-hood, which itself is a historically contingent condition rather than a natural one, contains our power of initiative and works its atomizing effects despite so many efforts to the contrary. Indeed, one must dig deep to identify and draw out certain hegemonies that are effective largely because they are so firmly engrained in our habitual ways of understanding. The argument, then, is foundational because it examines the historically produced conditions of social, political, and economic life with which people around the world must contend in one way or another. It is therefore also empirical insofar as it tries to understand the tangible legacies of colonial expansion, capitalist exploitation, scientific administration, and so on. In contrast, a reductionist argument would claim that all people are predetermined to respond to pregiven conditions in the same way and seek the same resolution to the conflicts they provoke. In demanding such homogeneity, a reductionist argument would probably resurrect old evolutionary theories of history that posited a singular trajectory to a teleological end point for the diverse peoples on earth. A foundational argument can recognize that these historically produced conditions themselves get instantiated differently depending on the times and places where they take hold, and that peoples' strategies for dealing with them also vary accordingly. But this situation does not lead to a countless number of local responses that share nothing in common. We are not confronted with a problem of hyper-relativism or absolute differences. Instead, the situation generates family resemblances between these different locations depending on how local actions absorbed, and were absorbed by, the broader historical processes in which they were situated. Each is thus intelligible to another; however, a singular end point is not predictable, desirable, or possible.

The book's argument is divided into three parts. Part 1 describes how the condition of migrant-hood is instantiated on a mass scale, in today's political, economic, and social realms and how migrant-hood renders people politically docile through atomization. This consigns them to a life of migrant-hood in two steps: (1) by pre-cluding the possibility of people mutually confirming each other's existence as particular people; and thus (2) by impeding joint political action between them whereby they would directly estab-lish their own sovereign forms, even within modest parameters. Denied their particular personhood, individuals are then absorbed into mass society through all three realms on the basis of their common animal features, through which they can only maintain "life itself." Despite the appearance of individualism displayed through postmodern consumer choice, these features render peo-ple identical specimens of a human species recognized only for a capacity to labor, both physically and cognitively.

Part 2 examines how the atomized world, particularly under neoliberalism, has become highly effective at connecting individu-alized people in never-ending economic and administrative pro-cesses. It furthermore seems to celebrate local initiatives realized through flexible, horizontal networks rather than transcendent, vertical structures. The basis of their connections, however, contin-ues to neglect people as particular individuals who could otherwise constitute their worlds and end the condition of migrant-hood. It thus continues to deny people as political beings. I argue that this trick of atomizing people through such connections works by priv-ileging one faculty of the mind over another, namely, the faculty of cognition, which seeks logical certainty in the abstract, over the faculty of thinking, which searches for meaning in the messiness of the empirical world. As occurred in mass society of the mid-twentieth century, neoliberalism requires cognition to propel its ceaseless economic and administrative activity, while discouraging thinking because it would question the meaning of the status quo itself. Thinking is destabilizing. The privileging of cognition has created a situation in which people have become highly *active* through their absorption into, and ambitious proliferation of, the global economy, while they remain unable to initiate political *action* because of continued atomization and loneliness. Thus, the site of the contemporary struggle for political appearance—in a word, freedom—resides at the boundary between the faculties of thinking and cognition, as the latter continues to underpin apparatuses of global rule.

Part 3 examines how the end of migrant-hood inaugurates the beginning of politics understood as the act of particular people directly constituting the worlds they jointly inhabit. This part begins by contrasting the technocracy of the concentration camp—the horrific extreme of modernity's capacity to rid people of political personhood—with the positive politics transpiring in spaces of appearance, precisely where thinking and willing actors constitute themselves, thereby inaugurating new beginnings and exercising the human power of initiative. A surprising, yet mundane, example of the latter is found in Primo Levi's description of his ten days with ten other inmates in the time between the Nazi evacuation of Auschwitz and the arrival of Soviet forces. I then go on to draw similarities between David Graeber's presentation of anarchism and Hannah Arendt's views on political action in order to clarify the conditions in which migrant-hood dissipates the moment people directly constitute spaces of appearance. It is here that atomized individuals obtain a worldly reality in the joint act of sovereign constitution, a joyful experience which resolves the existential question of whether the individual matters in this world.

PART 1   ATOMIZATION: THE UBIQUITOUS CONDITION OF MIGRANT-HOOD

Under the absolute government of a single man, despotism, to reach the soul, clumsily struck at the body, and the soul, escaping from such blows, rose gloriously above it; but in democratic republics that is not at all how tyranny behaves; it leaves the body alone and goes straight for the soul.

—Alexis de Tocqueville, *Democracy in America*

We conventionally understand the migration experience as one of anomie, alienation, and disorientation. Migrants are uprooted from an alleged homeland where all surroundings were pleasant, familiar, and consonant with their psychological disposition. We understand that people have their natural places on earth, the estrangement from which can only be a stressful experience. Imagine refugees fleeing political or natural disasters, hoping to find safety in the welcoming arms of another country, but never quite understanding the local customs. Consider the immigrant neighborhoods in major metropolises, where satellite television dishes angle toward news arriving from the home country (to say nothing of the traffic in cell phone calls). If immigrants themselves never fully integrate, then the host society likewise never fully accepts them. Even immigrants who naturalize (that is, make natural their new national identity), and even their descendents, often confront the suspicious question, "Yes, but where are you really from?" Defensive citizens talk of immigrants in catastrophic terms: they invade our homeland; they arrive in waves; they are like viruses in an otherwise healthy organism. Sympathetic citizens speak in patronizing terms to help smooth a migrant's integration through language-training opportunities, job-training workshops, cultural outreach events, and so on. In either case, difference conjures up fear: the nationalist rejects the difference, the liberal attempts to transform it into similarity, and the multiculturalist wants to cordon it off in its own isolated space. Meanwhile, the migrant encounters what appears as homogeneity and feels foreign.

But is the migrant's situation so different from the citizen's? If the migrant is a "virus" in the national organism, then the unemployed citizen is regarded as a "leech" on its welfare system. If the migrant is a foreigner who does not really belong, then the nonconforming citizen is dismissed as a misanthrope who does not really want to be with "us" anyway. The pressures on the citizen to "fit in" are strong. The immigrant who finally blends in by prospering economically is held up as a model citizen for what she has become—a good entrepreneur or a good worker—not for what she was before she arrived. The citizen is thus reminded of what she *should* be if she has not become so already. If an immigrant can do it, then certainly the citizen can too. Without such conformity, one risks social status, job offers, promotions, and other opportunities, or receiving the cold shoulder from peers and neighbors. Granted, conformity does not always appear as the mass conformity of the mid-twentieth century; it is now often niche-specific to match the more refined marketing strategies deployed in today's world of fragmented consumer identities. However, the general discomfort in national politics with migrants testifies to the endurance of traditional mass nationalism in contemporary identity politics. Ironically, as citizens exclude migrants, citizens themselves become rhetorically indistinguishable from each other because in the very act of marginalization lies the assumption that citizens themselves are fundamentally the same. In the end, to think and act in terms of "citizens" and "migrants" is to stereotype each side of the dichotomy.

This situation of homogenized political subjects creates an existential challenge in the form of denying particular persons places in the political realm, regardless of whether they are citizens or migrants. What is missing is not the chance to say what one thinks—today's social media provide countless opportunities to do that. Instead, the missing factor is the presence of another person to seriously listen and directly respond, as one political equal would to another. Lacking that, the possibility for people to constitute public spaces in direct negotiations with each other—that is, from the different standpoints they necessarily occupy in the world—is at best seriously obstructed, and at worst eliminated altogether. As we are not empowered to undergo this foundational political act, sovereignty is either constituted upon us (as abstract representatives of a nation) or against us (as migrants who do not belong "here"). Unlike the politics of nonstate societies, the particular individual does not confirm his existence through negotiations in a positive political realm. Instead, he is sequestered to the private realms of hobbies, business pursuits, and leisure, where he is free to enjoy himself, enrich himself, and no more. Though each citizen may vote and while each person remains "among men," none of them "count as one" because none are politically empowered as particular individuals. Part 1 unpacks how this disempowerment, which enables mass society as we know it, works against both the migrant and the citizen in the political, economic, and social contexts.

POLITICS: THE CITIZEN AND THE MIGRANT

To uncover the common platform on which the migrant and the citizen stand, we must ask how their dichotomization emerged. While neither term can be understood without the other, the birth of the modern "citizen" gave the "migrant" the sharp and abstract definition that we now know. Prior to the nation-state, "migrant" encapsulated a variety of people in motion, including pilgrims, exiles, traders, peasants working seasonally, and domestics working in one house then another. The people traveling in these circuits were not categorically defined as the "other," because they were not contrasted against an equally abstract category of "citizen": some people happened to be moving, while some people happened to be at home. Many of these travelers could benefit from local customs of hospitality. Rigid cosmological boundaries between inside and outside were not concretized in purist form as they would in the system of nation-states. Instead, most migrations were commonly understood as the routines of life in which anyone could be absorbed.

To grasp the sheer power of such an abstract category as citizen in shaping our collective imagination, one might ask a deceptively simple question suggested by Benedict Anderson: Of the millions of my fellow citizens, how many do I actually know? The question involves something different from a head count of one's friends and associates. It forces us to ask, on the one hand, how we come to identify with millions of people who will remain complete strangers to us, and on the other, to still look differently on the migrants whom we get to know on personal terms. The danger here is not simply that we might befriend a particular migrant rather than a particular citizen. Rather, it is the refusal to premise our ethics on the abstract categories of "citizen" and "migrant" in favor of assessing particular situations and persons. The primary political act within the confines of the nation-state system is to see the world in its particularity and then move to general, but fluid, ethical guidelines, rather than rely on abstract principles to instruct us in dealing with people in the particular. In contrast, the citizen-migrant dichotomy reduces complexity, diversity, and particularity to trite differences of "culture" stereotypically understood. The point here is not that the concept of the nation is insignificant for people on a deeply personal level; rather, the problem is that the concept so dominates how we understand complexity and difference that we fail to let the world speak to us in its own terms. It flattens how we see ourselves and others, and so limits the possible ways we can engage the world around us. The problem began at the end of the eighteenth century when the very emergence of that which liberated people from feudalism and royal whim also became the initial condition of modern migrant-hood: the birth of the nation.

The migrant-citizen dichotomy only makes sense relative to the modern nation-state. France became the first nation proper when its 1789 revolution, the definitive revolution of modern times, became defined as a popular movement undertaken in the name of the suffering masses. The masses became the "people" understood as the nation in whose name the republic—*res publica*, or public thing—was called into existence. The category "people" did not apply universally to all people on earth, but rather it indicated a delimited category of nationals who became the French citizenry. Moreover, people were not understood as an eclectic group of particular individuals, but rather as a mass of living beings who shared the same national essence and the immediate biological demand for bread. Reduced to a singular national entity that could theoretically speak in one voice, they would thus be spoken for by a revolutionary elite who tested political rivals' loyalty to the revolution by the extent to which those rivals demonstrated their compassion for the "people." Political legitimacy was now rooted in an earthly abstraction, which cannot in actuality speak, rather than a divine one. The American Revolution, occurring just a few years earlier, did not transpire in the name of the people qua homogenized mass. "We the people" in the Declaration of Independence assumed a heterogeneous public and the revolutionary leadership originally had aimed only at restoring the colonies' governing powers usurped by the monarchy. Its aim compared modestly to what became of the French Revolution, namely, nothing short of an attempt to completely reorganize society. (Indeed, the

French Revolution completely changed the original political meaning of the word "revolution," which had adhered to the astronomical definition: a full-circle return to a previously occupied position rather than the beginning of something fundamentally new.) By the early nineteenth century, however, the United States would begin to adopt a homogenous concept of the nation similar to the French. Boorstin relates how U.S. nation-building began with the apotheosis of George Washington as its mythical founding father within months after his death in December 1799. Mason Locke Weems, a salesman and an Anglican priest, presented Washington after his death as a man of saintly virtue who could unite a new and diverse nation, even though he had been a highly controversial politician during his life. From that point until the Civil War, the cult of George Washington grew to consume the United States and established him as the mythical father of the national family.

The newly emerged American and French nations signified "civic" nations, which meant that any individual could join them as long as the would-be citizen adopted the national language and culture. The concept of the civic nation made sense at a historical moment in which "humanity" was being discovered. The Age of Enlightenment demanded a radical equality based on the universal capacity for human reason, thus eliminating differences based on religion and inherited social rank. Nevertheless, a certain ambiguity lurked in this new apparent freedom. Did it mean that people could deploy reason to govern their own affairs or, much differently, that people could only deploy it to adapt themselves to the supposed natural direction of history that intellectuals would claim to discover? The former empowers people to constitute themselves in a body politic rather, per the latter, than submit to being governed as categorical types that behave according to some allegedly intrinsic law of motion or history. The latter interpretation would swiftly take priority, but in either case no reason remained to explain why the life of a monarch, ruling by divine right, should be valued more highly than that of a peasant or any-one else. The old argument required a particular Christian belief in which salvation was a gift of the afterlife. The new, modern thinking demanded salvation here on earth and during this life-time. This salvation meant freedom from misery and poverty. Indeed, the appeal of modernity has always been its promise to liberate humanity from all possible forms of suffering. However, its definitive limit has also been that which made it so distinctively unprecedented: its radical insistence that each person is funda-mentally equal. This equality did not refer to political equality among qualitatively different people, but rather an equality which assumes that all people are fundamentally the same. The abstrac-tions that would underpin modern political order—such as the "people," "nation," "working class," and now "humanity"—fail to make sense without the latter understanding of equality. To this problem, we can add the paradox of maintaining national identity in the post–Cold War age of humanity: while nationalism assumes that each nation differs fundamentally, humanitarianism assumes that all people are the same regardless of their national origin.

Indeed, the contradiction between nation and humanity (as opposed to the abstract citizen versus the particular speaking sub-ject) crystallized quickly as Napoleon swept eastward across Europe to spread the virtues of the French Enlightenment. If he fought his wars in the name of a common humanity (while seeing himself as its savior), then surely the diverse peoples of Europe would want to join the French civic nation. (Postwar American hegemony oper-ated on the same contradictory template as did the left-wing revo-lutionary aims of the Soviet Union. Surely everyone would want to be either an American or a member of the international working class.) Of course, the peoples of central Europe showed little inter-est in getting absorbed into a French style of universalism. After their own liberation from ancient dynasties, they sought to root themselves in their own linguistic and cultural traditions. They developed the concept of the "ethnic" nation, whose tenets were best articulated by the German linguist Gottfried Herder. Ethnic nationalists found French civic nationalism void of substance and devoid of what people needed in a new, disorienting modern world: a place to call one's own. If anyone on the European continent could be French, then what was so special about the honor? Opponents of the French model decried it as a form of rootless cosmopolitanism based on imperial interests rather than one's particular cultural identity. (Today's debates between "globalism" and "localism," or "secularism" and "fundamentalism" operate on the same template.) Central Europeans sought substantive community on the basis of common language, unique ties to the surrounding lands, shared mythologies, and fictionalized kinships testifying to their own particularity and exclusivity. Ethnic nationalism recognized particular groups of people as organic parts of the land, and each member of the ethnic group obtained the cultural essence from this "mother's milk." Strictly speaking, a migrant could not be absorbed into the "ethnic" nation because membership was a matter of blood and organic ties to the land, not a social contract.

It is deceptively simple to dismiss the ethnic nation as closed and argue that the civic nation is open. Despite their differences, both the civic and the ethnic nation draw sharp boundaries, carry historical racist baggage, and insist on their norms (even in today's pastiche, postmodern world). Their similar exclusionary effects result from the premise that "people" is synonymous with a national mass in which individuals share the same fundamental traits despite differences that might appear on the surface. In both ethnic and civic nations, the individual qua particular person is secondary to the individual qua embodiment of the nation. Membership in either requires that one internalize a national essence as the core of one's person, thereby nullifying the presence of particular individuals as political subjects themselves. The civic nation assumed cultural homogeneity as it emerged in the particular cultural contexts of France as well as Britain and British North America. Immigration remains highly controversial in civic nations such as Britain, France, the United States, and Australia. Though Canada has recorded a greater than fifty percent popular approval rating for immigration, this figure likely is achieved by the low levels of illegal immigration in this less geographically accessible country. Moreover, the naturalization laws of the European Union's "ethnic" nation-states are basically the same as those of its western "civic" nation-states. If a permanent visa is granted, then for citizenship both require a residency period (usually about five years), the passing of a language exam, the passing of a civics or culture exam, and proof of income. Over centuries the creation of civic and ethnic nations required enormous cultural destruction through the elimination of other European languages and dialects that either did not get standardized in school curriculums or could not find patrons among the political and literary elites engaged in nation-building. If therefore civic nations are not as free of prejudice as their citizens might boast, then ethnic nations were never as homogenous as their national folklore implies. Neither the civic nor the ethnic nation could maintain its logical consistency without systematically denying the quirks, contingencies, and plurality of lived history.

The dependency of the modern nation (civic or ethnic) on persons in the abstract and its unease with persons in the particular comes into full relief when we compare the memorialization of ancient and modern war heroes. Homer regularly describes both Greek and Trojan soldiers as particular people tied to, or descending from, other particular people from particular places:

> Each man slew his man in the broken field:
> Hektor killed Stikhíos and Arkesílaös,
> one a Boiotian captain, and the other
> comrade of brave Menéstheus; then Aineías
> dispatched Medôn and Iasos: the first-named
> a bastard son of Oïleus, and half-brother
> of Aïas: he had lived in Phylakê
> in exile from his own land, having murdered
> a kinsman of his stepmother, Eriôpis.

Iasos was a captain of Athenians
and son, so called, of Sphêlos Boukólidês.
Poulýdamas killed Mékisteus—Ekhíos,
his father, fell in the early battle line
before Polítês—and heroic Agênor
killed Kloníos. As Dëïokhos ran,
Paris hit his shoulder from behind
and drove the brazen spearhead through his chest.[1]

Heroes of the ancient world were rewarded with immortality. This did not grant an extension of biological life beyond a mortal death; rather, it located the person in historical memory and recognized his unique effect on the polis and on his peers. The ready example in the Western tradition is Akhilleus, who distinguished himself on the battlefield by bravely leading men and completing great missions in ways that only he could. Greek history moved in unpredictable directions because of his own interventions, testifying to the particularity of his person. Likewise, Homer's *Iliad* and other Greek stories preserve Akhilleus as a particular person, not as the quintessential Greek. If he had been, there would be no need to preserve his particular legacy. Other soldiers would have proved themselves his equal (that is, the same as him) and so no Greek in particular would need be remembered beyond his mortal life. However, Akhilleus' life needed to carry on after his body perished because his unique personhood partially constituted the Greek world itself.

Therefore, the funeral rite's crucial importance is that ensconces the particular person in the collective memory of the living, as much as it prepares a soul for an afterlife. In this regard, Akhilleus would have committed the gravest injustice to the Trojans had he not returned Hektor's body to his father, Priam. Such pettiness would have denied Troy its chance to immortalize Hektor into Trojan lore, through the funeral ceremony, and so (re)constitute its polity as the particular place it had become by virtue of his

---

1. From the *Iliad*, translation by Robert Fitzgerald (Anchor, 1974).

particular actions. Despite Akhilleus' rage at Hektor for killing Patrokles, for him to deny Troy the funeral ceremony, through which the Trojans could actualize their very *being* as Trojans, would have been proportionately beyond the loss that Akhilleus himself had suffered. It made no difference that twelve days later, after Hektor's funeral ceremony ended, the Greek armies would raze Troy, slaughter its men, and enslave its women and children. Indeed, the purpose of holding the ceremony in light of Troy's imminent demise would be lost in the modern world, because the sacking of Troy was not about an eradication of a people from the surface of the earth (the concern of modern warfare). Likewise, it was not about removing the Trojan people from living memory, but only about Agamemnon exacting revenge on Paris for the particular act of seducing and abducting Helen, the wife of his brother Meneláos. It was fought for the sake of honor between particular people rather than as an eternal battle between two abstract nations.

The ultimate war hero of modern society, in contrast, is not the great general recorded in national histories. Rather, it is the unknown soldier, in whose monumental tomb burns an eternal flame to remember him not as a particular person but as the embodiment of the nation that must never die. Eternity preserves abstractions like nations and souls. Immortality, on the other hand, preserves the particular person. In contemporary society we would likely describe a quest for immortality as arrogant. The charge might well be warranted if the desire rested on the belief that one was morally superior to one's peers, but not if one simply strived to be recognized among others as a particular person whose presence had left a constituent and enduring mark on the polis. Particularity is not absolute superiority but rather about differences that distinguish one individual from another. While Akhilleus is immortalized as the greatest soldier and runner, Odysseus is immortalized as the cleverest tactician.

The funeral of the unknown soldier does not (and cannot) recognize the particular individual in the grave. If it did, then the ceremony would negate the purpose of the national monument erected on it, namely, to perpetuate the abstract nation above all else, even though the monuments themselves betray a sadness for the loss of an unacknowledged particular life. To achieve this goal, the tomb of the unknown soldier is given the most moving, memorable, and conspicuous design in the cemetery so as to remind the viewer that no matter who falls we are all citizens of the eternal nation. The known soldiers are buried in impersonal geometrical rows with identical headstones (often in the shape of white crosses) lest the particular name inscribed on them take priority over the collectivized nation for whom these particular soldiers fell. Viewing the graves of known soldiers, their white headstones neatly aligned, one imagines tragic faceless bodies falling like waves of dominoes across the battlefield.

The effect of acknowledging people only as identical representatives of the nation is that it negates the particular person's political voice. For if each individual is conceptualized as the carrier of a national essence, then it makes no difference who speaks because no one in particular needs to speak. If all are the same, then *any* given individual can speak as long as no one speaks *as* a particular individual. The politician or technocratic elite is just as capable of speaking for the masses as anyone else as long as they speak in the language of "common sense." National leaders thus appear indistinguishable from the nation, which cannot be said about Akhilleus with respect to the Greeks or Hektor with respect to the Trojans. It was their individuality that made them so vitally important to the lives of others.

The upshot for the anonymous citizen is that a circular foundation to mass national society materializes: a plurality of people inhabit a particular parcel of land, which in time gets identified as the "nation," which then defines the original sovereign population, and which has thus reduced a plurality of people to an abstract thing. While this circle necessarily erases particular differences as it generates a homogenous national identity, it likewise homogenizes all external individuals as "foreigners." It insists on an unbridgeable divide between the "citizen" and the "migrant," between "us" and "them." It thus seems natural that this border be carefully regulated as a matter of national-cum-territorial security understood as an existential problem as much as a logistical one. To be sure, the citizen gains liberation from tyranny and misery, but to define this liberation in the name of an abstract nation was to ensure that politics and revolution would also engender a great loss. Specifically, that loss was a place where particular individuals could constitute with others as their own. Political empowerment of any person cannot exist without the recognition of all persons as fundamentally different.

In this historical trajectory, politics becomes mass party politics, which after the thrill of the revolution subsides, creates a frustrating situation in which party elites become ever more estranged from the masses they represent. The estranged relationship between those holding the levers of power and those to whom power is addressed is mediated through abstract representations of the "voters," whose input has been reduced to the passive processes of responding to surveys, participating in focus groups, and dropping ballots in boxes. In this context, political movements around the world often adopt similarly antiparty stances in favor of egalitarian organizational forms that acknowledge the eclecticism of their supporters. Party politics has shown itself unable to give people, qua particular individuals, the voice that being a participant in politics requires. It is thus reasonable that Brazilian activists, protesting current living conditions and cutbacks to social services ahead of the 2014 World Cup and the 2016 Summer Olympics, made clear that they belong to no political party (84% according to one BBC report). Their frustration results not necessarily from a political party's incompetence, but rather from the desire of people to take direct control of the conditions of their lives.

If the citizen is estranged from politics in the positive sense of the term, then we can hardly distinguish him from the migrant, who can be legitimately excluded from politics altogether. What is at stake is not precisely one's material quality of life, but rather the capacity to engage others from one's particular standpoint and so constitute public space in the very act. Like interest groups for any citizen, migrant associations lobby for improved living and working conditions. Yet regardless of success, their initiatives do not create a polity in which the migrant can appear as a particular individual; the migrant remains a category to be managed as a legal or policy problem. The difference between the citizen and the migrant in the political context is that the former has a more secure legal access to basic life requirements in the form of social services, guaranteed legal protection for general well-being, and enhanced voting rights. Notably, however, a relatively wealthy migrant will still enjoy a much greater quality of life than a relatively poor citizen, because liberal society today is organized first on the basis of safeguarding private interests. This situation works to the advantage of the well resourced more than it does to that of the citizen per se. Yet in either case economic success does not result in political empowerment positively understood.

ECONOMY: THE SLAVE (AND THE) LABORER

The slavery that emerged in early modern capitalism and the subsequent spread of industrial labor reinforced migrant-hood as a modern condition. This effect paralleled what occurred with the rise of the nation-state: as the generic national, rather than the particular person, premises modern sovereignty, so the generic (or abstract) laborer, rather than the skilled artisan, premises the modern economy. Slavery and labor share crucial fundamental qualities, which render people interchangeable in the labor force and so exchangeable for a market price. The transition from slavery to labor did not inaugurate a political liberation as such, but only a new ethic on preserving and strengthening the individual's capacity to labor and, in later years, to consume. (Lacking income, a slave cannot be a consumer.) Hence, the body and mind were to be nurtured for economic purposes rather than neglected, let alone brutalized. In effect, however, individuals remain commodities to be bought and sold on the labor market. The difference is only in the manner in which the buyer purchases labor power: the slave's labor power is obtained by purchasing his body from a separate owner, while the laborer owns his body but sells his labor power to an employer. Either way, to reduce particular individuals as subjects, endowed with the capacity to speak, to individuals as objects, groomed with skill sets valued for their utilitarian functions, subordinates them to the economic processes that they serve. Unlike artisans, who directly control and uniquely define the production process and leave their signature in (not just on) the finished product, the slave and the laborer lack any such control over that process and so leave no particular mark on its result.

Three enduring qualities of slavery likewise premise the modern laborer's condition of migrant-hood. The first is temporal. Slaves primarily conducted labor that did not leave a trace on the wider world. This labor characteristically involved the planting and harvesting of food that would be immediately consumed upon production, activity that was predicated on the body's and nature's circular time clocks. As nothing endured from what was produced, the life of a slave was embodied in Camus's Sisyphean task: once complete, the process restarts from where it began, trapping the slave in a never-ending cycle of production simply for consumption's sake. Historically, "labor" refers to any of the repetitive chores necessary to ensure bare biological survival of the private household: the growth of food, cleaning and maintenance of the home, and childbirth. Furthermore, like childbirth, labor of any kind has always been associated with the pain it imposes on the body and with its tethering to the body's metabolic cycles to ensure survival from one day to the next and from one generation to the next. Limited to this context, the life of a slave becomes indistinguishable from the life of an animal, as both are locked in circular time, being chained to the imminent demands of their metabolism; both are reduced to representative specimens of a species; and neither have the capacity to constitute public space (that is, engage in a fully human, political life). It should be clear that this point does not define slave as a particular person, but rather the essence of the structural position from which the particular slave must negotiate her existence. The structure of this situation scarcely differs from the laborer even if the latter obtains compensation through a wage rather than through the food she grows. Both the slave and the laborer are subordinated to the rhythm of economic processes as they try to maintain the cyclical needs of their biology, which in turns provides the material foundation to society.

The second quality is spatial. Slaves and women were confined to the household, which was spatially and socially segregated from public places where issues of importance for the polity were discussed. This spatial prohibition had a significant temporal effect. The result of a public appearance was the actualization of the particular person in the eyes of his peers during political deliberations. This appearance, denied to the slave, moved history through rectilinear time rather than biological-cum-circular time, because the articulation of speaking subjects' particular perspectives, if it leads to action, inaugurates new and unprecedented directions. Hence, in the distinction between "man" as an animal and "man" as a political actor (*zöe* and *bios* respectively in the ancient Greek differentiation of these two subject positions), only the latter can appear in a public space to be recognized as a particular person in the eyes of others. Modern laborers face the same situation, although it manifests differently: they are not precluded from leaving private space. This Greek prohibition, in effect, is not necessary because there is no public space from which to prohibit them, as they are unable to constitute public space by virtue of the denial of their particular personhood. There is thus no need to confine anyone to a private sphere.

The third quality is instrumental. Chattel slavery involves more than the physical coercion of people to labor against their will. If chattel slavery was to help integrate a budding, global economy, then it required the slave's "objectification": the slave/laborer is recognized only as an object composed of skills that can be expressed monetarily on an exchange market or deployed to valorize the owner's capital investment in the slave/laborer. Once the particular speaking subject is silenced, the remaining animalized object, again, is subordinated to the economic processes it serves. Instruments, like objects, cannot publicly discuss the ethics of those processes, as this would elevate them to speaking subjects with a place in the political world where they could express judgments about the injustices they confront. As a speechless object is politically inanimate, no consequence need be feared for doing violence to it. Of course, slaves can push back either in subtle forms of passive resistance or in open rebellion. These events testify to the ultimately indomitable human spirit. However, the fact that the spirit cannot be destroyed does not change the empirical fact that the configuration of social relations is strongly structured against the slave so as to contain the spirit as much as possible. The liberal-cum-socialist achievement that has outlawed slavery and limited the exploitation of the working class succeeded primarily in protecting the laborer's body. It did not fundamentally give the laborer a political voice in which she speaks as a particular individual—that which distinguishes her from all other individuals.

Aristotle reasoned that a master and slave have nothing in common and so justice cannot exist between them. He concluded that a slave is a tool without a soul while a tool is a slave without a soul. Aristotle did not see the soul as distinct from the body, but rather that the soul is actualized when the activities conducted by the body are done well. The craftsman thus actualizes himself in all his virtuosity in the act of crafting his object. The slave has no such opportunity because he performs no craft. He controls no process of becoming (as the wood becomes a table through the carpenter's hand), because he himself is controlled by productive processes, primarily agriculture. As he lacks a soul, there is no friendship and hence no parity between slave and master. Unsettling as it is to contemporary ears, we can leave aside Aristotle's assertion in *Nicomachean Ethics* that slaves lack souls, and similarly in *Politics* that they lack reason even though they can follow reason when commanded, if we interpret him in light of one's structural position in the production process. In a modern context, the absence of a soul and a capacity to logically follow commands still indicate the absence of the particular speaking subject and hence the presence of the slave. For Aristotle makes clear in *Politics* that slavery allows the master to avoid menial tasks so that he can attend to higher matters of politics and philosophy in which he is afforded time, respectively, to speak as his own person and to think about the world that he is shaping. The operative political point that we can take is not that of human nature confining us to the circumscribed lives of slaves or women, but rather that attending to the circular demands of production and consumption robs us of the opportunity to become political agents in the sense of (re)constituting the polity. If Aristotle were to speak of reason and slavery in a modern idiom, he would have to conclude that everyone is a slave and there is no political sphere into which we can enter.

As Foucauldian scholars well know, the shift out of slavery— and general shift away from discipline as negative sanction—redefined the mechanisms of modern power relations. In the case of slavery, the incentive to labor is external to the body and negative to the person through threat of physical force. In the case of the wage laborer, the impetus is positive and internal to the individual through the notion that labor is what makes us self-sufficient. Refusing to work does not risk physical punishment but only access to a vital wage. Thus, the wage laborer has been identified as "free labor" on the rhetorical assumption that he can move about the land to pick and choose the best contract. This interpretation sustains today's neoliberal logic, as each worker is said to possess a skill set which he invests in a job, however temporary, to retrieve profit in the form of a wage or, simply, work experience. The freedom of choice allegedly sits in the worker's own hands. However, despite a change in the mechanism of power relations, the essence of labor relations has hardly dissipated with the collapse of slavery as a formal institution. Atomization and alienation of the laboring body has arguably been taken to a higher and far more efficient level. Most significantly, rather than systematically destroy the body, labor practices now are designed to protect and even enhance its laboring capacities through ergonomic machinery, safety equipment, job training, and healthier working conditions. This approach enables greater productivity from the workforce, while wage remuneration creates a consumer class out of it. As capitalism needs constant consumption, it cannot afford to maintain a slaving population that has no credit or cash on hand to spend. None of this, however, is tantamount to political empowerment as such because individuals are reduced to the tasks of maintaining their bodies and their social statuses, that is, the monotony of biological and social reproduction as ends in themselves. In *Early Manuscripts*, Marx quotes Buret to drive home this point, which still holds true today even if contemporary laboring conditions have improved since the nineteenth century: "Labour is life, and if life is not exchanged every day for food it soon suffers and perishes. If the life of man is to be a commodity, then slavery must be acknowledged." We have not yet found our way out of this sad equation, but only more sophisticated smokescreens to blur its accuracy.

Furthermore, the economic basis to the condition of migranthood permeates the entire workforce—blue-collar and white-collar— as both are valued for instrumental purposes only. Marx again proves contemporary in noting that while the laborer becomes a slave to his labor power, the capitalist becomes a slave to his investment because "the immanent laws of capitalist production confront the individual capitalist as a coercive force external to him." While the capitalist enjoys greater monetary reward, she must rely not only on blue-collar physical labor but also on white-collar cognitive labor. That white-collar labor performs a wide range of cognitive tasks designed to ensure the greatest possible return for the lowest possible investment. These range from accounting to investing, predicting growth trends, risk assessment, marketing, and logistics. These activities similarly characterize administrative work in the public sector, which strives to sustain a population capable of laboring and consuming at the lowest possible social cost.

The laborer's physical activities and the white-collar worker's cognitive activities share something fundamentally in common. Any given person can perform either activity because these are not dependent on a particular individual's unique standpoint in the world. Rather, they depend on the mere existence of the human animal to labor physically with the body (blue-collar) or to perform procedures of abstract logic with the mind (white-collar). Any individual endowed with a body or a mind can be trained to perform these functions, even if some can do them more efficiently than others, because they do not require the particular subject's ethical assessment. For this reason, both white-collar and blue-collar laborers face stiff competition from other workers from whom they cannot distinguish themselves and from machines and algorithmic programs that can duplicate their respective functions. Such equality in the labor market bears an uncanny resemblance to equality in the political sphere, specifically, that all people are equal, homogenous, dispensable, exchangeable, and so need not speak. Independent of any given person, economic processes continue unthreatened.

In sum, the quintessential characteristics of the slave and the white-collar or blue-collar laborer are their entrapment in circular time; their inability to constitute a public space in which to appear as a particular person; and their objectification and instrumentalization necessary to achieve economic growth on a mass scale.

While slavery has been abolished, the practice of labor still contains the laborer in the same position of speechlessness. Rather than being bought and sold as an object, the modern laborer endeavors to sell himself (his labor power) and so consents to his own objectification. Confinement to the objectified status and the lack of a space in which to appear as a particular speaking subject eliminate the possibility for political action. This situation results in individuals necessarily consumed with work but detached from anything durable of which they themselves are constituent parts. One might conclude that while modern economics treats the laborer's body with kid gloves in comparison to the slave's body, it does an even graver injustice to the former's character by creating a situation in which he will rationally and willingly agree to reduce himself to an instrumentalized object. It is difficult to imagine a slave giving up his spirit even if he must give up his body.

Beckett's tragicomic insight on this point in *Waiting for Godot* appears in the relationship between Pozzo, a liberal donning the air of a gentleman, and Lucky, his dutiful assistant who, unlike a slave, internalizes his own oppression. By means of a rope tied around his neck, Lucky obediently pulls Pozzo along a road to nowhere. Together they are the unrooted bourgeois migrants of capitalist society. He responds to Pozzo's every condescending, monosyllabic command and unfailingly holds his bags even when they are at a standstill. He speaks only once throughout the entire play in what amounts to a lengthy train of jumbled thoughts that would appear as educated speech if not heard with full attention. They encounter the bystanders Estragon and Vladimir who, waiting in vain for a man named Godot, are stationary migrants. Attached to nothing but themselves, they rarely leave the scene as time passes them by. They wish to know why Lucky does not put down Pozzo's bags to make himself more comfortable. Pozzo unequivocally explains:

> Why he doesn't make himself comfortable? Let's try and get this clear. Has he not the right to? Certainly he has. It follows that he doesn't want

to. There's reasoning for you. And why doesn't he want to? (*Pause.*) Gentlemen, the reason is this. . . . He wants to impress me, so that I'll keep him. . . . He imagines that when I see how well he carries I'll be tempted to keep him on in that capacity. . . . He imagines that when I see him indefatigable I'll regret my decision [to get rid of him]. Such is his miserable scheme. As though I were short of slaves! . . . Remark that I might just as well have been in his shoes than mine and he in mine. If chance had not willed otherwise. To each one his due. . . . But instead of driving him away as I might have done, I mean instead of simply kicking him out on his arse, in the goodness of my heart I am bringing him to the fair, where I hope to get a good price for him. The truth is you can't drive such creatures away. The best thing would be to kill them. (*Lucky weeps.*)

SOCIETY: THE BANISHED

Banishment signified a devastating form of punishment in polities organized on the basis of customs, like those migrating "out of Africa." It strictly segregated the individual from the polity through the individual's dismissal from family, lineage, or village or town altogether. This presented an obvious difficulty in meeting one's biological needs, as food acquisition was so often a task coordinated among groups of hunters, gatherers, or farmers. Securing food involved cooperation in its storage, trade, and preparation. Yet such polities were never as self-contained as assumed from a contemporary standpoint. Other networks and alliances linked people across considerable geographic distances and offered them connections to other villages. The banished individual might still manage to meet basic needs if he was savvy enough. Perhaps the banished was still permitted to stay at his home village, but others were forbidden from establishing eye contact with him. In any case, banishment loomed as the supreme punishment for transgression because it rendered the particular individual invisible to everyone and reduced him to the living dead. The intended effect of banishment would not necessarily have been to kill the banished through isolation in the wilderness. A simple death sentence would have expedited this goal. The point was to rob the banished of his very identity by forbidding others to recognize it. Tocqueville best synopsized the significance of lost recognition: one might still remain among men, but lose one's rights to count as one, that is, to live a life worse than death. The body may carry on in its generic, animal functions, but the existence of the particular character conveyed through that body can be confirmed by no one.

The tale of Odysseus on his return from the Trojan War well illustrates the isolation of the unrecognized individual. In drawing the wrath of Poseidon, Odysseus is forced to journey for twenty years across the seas and on islands where no one recognizes him as the hero he has become. Naked and destitute, he arrives anonymously on the island of Skhería, where the young girl Nausikaa, daughter oft Prince Alkínoös and Princess Arêtê, stumbles upon him and mentions his presence to her father. Mostly likely, Odysseus never asserts his identity because no one would have believed that such a great figure would have arrived in such a decrepit condition. The prince nevertheless agrees to accommodate Odysseus, according to the custom of hosting travelers, and on his departure organizes a banquet for him without having yet learned his true identity. A minstrel's song during the banquet tells the tale of the Trojan Horse, an exploit that Odysseus had masterminded. During the song, tears well up in Odysseus' eyes confirming his true identity to Alkínoös who soon demands that Odysseus declare himself. Odysseus himself has suggested the song to the minstrel perhaps as a way to provoke his own emotional response. (Again, he is known as the cleverest tactician.) Odysseus' display of raw emotion should be read as more than just frustrated vanity resulting from his inability to claim credit for his wartime exploit. Despite Odysseus' considerable vanity displayed in other episodes, Homer's description of the scene indicates something quite different:

> And Odysseus,
> let the bright molten tears run down his cheeks,
> weeping the way a wife mourns for her lord
> on the lost field where he has gone down fighting
> the day of wrath that came upon his children.
> At sight of the man panting and dying there,
> she slips down to enfold him, crying out;
> then feels the spears, prodding her back and shoulders,
> and goes bound into slavery and grief.
> Piteous weeping wears away her cheeks:
> but no more piteous than Odysseus' tears,
> cloaked as they were, now, from the company.[2]

The equation of Odysseus with a now widowed wife conveys the loss of personhood through lack of recognition from another person. The exploit of the Trojan Horse embodied a singular act in war that recast the direction of history, an act that only he could have initiated in the company of others, which would be preserved in collective memory. As with Hektor and Akhilleus, that act, now narrated in folklore across the Greek islands, constituted Odysseus as the particular person he was in the eyes of his peers and granted him an immortal presence in the world. Yet condemned to migrant-hood by Poseidon, he could not be identified with the story by which others could recognize him.

That the widowed wife feels the spear in her back prodding her into slavery suggests the feminist insight that a woman's identity and status was tied to her husband: if he dies in war, then the victor is entitled to carry her away as the prize. Yet Homer is not just reminding us of women's secondary status or, in stereotypical terms, trying to effeminize an otherwise masculine figure. Furthermore, Odysseus is not compared to an enslaved widow because he himself is about to be enslaved as a war prize; rather, Odysseus, like the enslaved widow, has no one who can confirm his personhood. Just

---

2. Passages from the *Odyssey* are from the translation by Robert Fitz-
ld (Vintage, 1990).

as the wife requires the husband to give her social status—a place in the world—Odysseus requires that someone recognize him as the particular person he showed himself to be in the Trojan War: both the widow and Odysseus are anonymous, non-persons. His grief results from being conscience that he, like a slave, is condemned to a life of solitary confinement even in the presence of other people. If he was a hero in the Trojan War, then for much of the *Odyssey* he lives under the condition of migrant-hood. Alkínoös gives Odysseus the chance to restore his identity when, on seeing him weep, he orders the minstrel to stop singing and, in return for hosting Odysseus like a brother, insists that Odysseus declare himself:

> We had prepared here, on our friend's behalf,
> safe conduct in a ship, and gifts to cheer him,
> holding that any man with a grain of wit
> will treat a decent suppliant as a brother.
> Now by the same rule, friend, you must not be
> secretive any longer! Come, in fairness,
> tell me the name you bore in that far off country;
> how were you known to family, and neighbors?
> No man is nameless – no man, good or bad,
> but gets a name in his first infancy,
> none being born, unless a mother bears him!

Odysseus then proceeds to tell of his wayward journey back from the Trojan War. However, Odysseus could only have regained his identity through Alkínoös recognizing him as the person who appears in the tales that had spread across the Greek world. Alkínoös therefore restored for Odysseus his place in that world and elevated him from the living dead to the living.

Why don't we have banishment as a form of punishment in mass society? The answer to the question is supplied by a question in return: from whom and to where would one be banished? One cannot be removed to another nation-state because the state performing the ban cannot force another state to accept the banished. Neither can the banished individual be barred from contact with other people because in the modern nation-state no one has an obligation to recognize you as a particular person. Outside of friendship, contacts are utilitarian and thus based on one's technical skills rather than one's ethical judgments. Those contacts are designed to be broken in any case. In modern society, one can almost maintain the body without a substantial connection to another person. Work can be conducted remotely, in isolation, or in a role in which substantial connection between employees is not required. Food acquisition transpires in a grocery store. One needs no connection to the cashier, who simply functions as an extension of the cash register itself (and is now replaceable through automated checkout). The individual is a priori deprived of a public in which to appear, so banishment becomes unimaginable as a punishment.

If banishment stood out in the nonmodern context because participation in the public realm and joint action underpin worldly order, then conversely, public action among particular individuals stands out in a modern context because banishment keeps order in tact. Coetzee illustrates these interconnected points in *Waiting for the Barbarians*. The novel tells of the isolation and punishment of an imperial magistrate living and working in a remote outpost where not much of importance happens. His troubles begin when he invites a visiting bureaucrat, Colonel Joll, from the imperial capital to see the indigenous fishing methods used by the villagers living in the adjacent lands. The magistrate explains soon afterward that two barbarian prisoners—an old man and a young boy suspected of insurgency—had engaged in nothing more than petty theft to compensate for their impoverished circumstances. However, the magistrate concludes that his explanation sounds more like a plea for the two captives, and indeed, Joll claims to have intelligence that the "barbarians" are preparing an attack. The magistrate's loyalty to the Empire is now in doubt. After Joll leaves, the magistrate begins living with a "barbarian" girl, whom Joll's associates had tortured, and eventually returns her home to her people. Joll, along with his force, later returns to the outpost with several more barbarian captives, and he then detains the magistrate for abandoning his post to return the girl and for fraternizing with the enemy. Afterward, Joll parades the barbarian captives in the main square and begins a ceremony of torture and humiliation with the townsfolk gathered around. The magistrate, managing to escape from his cell, works his way through the crowd and musters up the courage to call out in the captives' defense.

To Joll he asserts, "*You!* You are depraving these people!" A soldier beats the magistrate to the ground in reply. He arises but then collapses on his knees in front of a sergeant, who beats him on his head and shoulders. Joll then approaches him with a hammer cradled in his hand. The magistrate shouts, "not with that! . . . you would not use a hammer on a beast, not on a beast!" He then hurls the sergeant from him. Determined to finish what he was saying, he narrates that "Godlike strength is mine. In a minute it will pass: Let me use it while it lasts." Then, to anyone who would listen, he calls out, "Look! . . . We are the great miracle of creation! But from some blows this miraculous body cannot repair itself! How—! . . . Look at these men. . . . *Men!*" For his outburst, the imperial police deprive him of food and water, torture him, and hang him in the square, first by his neck, though the noose is loose enough to prevent strangulation, and then by his hands, which are tied behind his back. (Like banishment, the point of torture is not to kill but only to indefinitely extend the liminal phase between life and death so that the victim's complete vulnerability in front of transcendent sovereign power becomes clear.) The townsfolk do not intervene in the gruesome spectacle even when he himself, whom they all know, is the target. Nevertheless, the magistrate is ultimately allowed to walk free. The imperial police well know that he cannot instigate political action because he now appears to the townsfolk as an animalized buffoon only worthy of pity.

However, the novel's key point is readily missed if the reader focuses too much on the magistrate. Banishment requires the cooperation of others to enforce it. The townsfolk accepted his internal banishment, and throughout the novel they usually appear as ephemeral, ghostly figures floating around the town, often in its marginal spaces. Banishment, then, did not distinguish the magistrate from the other townsfolk, who never publicly assert themselves at any point in the story. They were already internally banished insofar as they were denied public appearance or, arguably, denied themselves such an appearance. The magistrate only differed from them insofar as he attempted to speak in his own voice in order to constitute a public with them, for which he was subsequently tortured. After much desperation, he dared to try to end his banishment even though he ultimately felt embarrassment for attempting what he later describes as a useless and meek outburst. Yet speak he did, and in so doing, he declared the validity of another's right to exist.

The magistrate's outburst does not mean that he necessarily understood the "barbarians," but only that he recognized them as actual people, not demonic stereotypes. Indeed, he must if he was to create a public space in which he himself could appear. To appear before others as an equal, one must see others as equally human. Rather than heroism, it was therefore a mundane act of trying to forge a place for himself in a world of which he himself could tolerate being a part. Before he acted against the ceremony of torture, he narrated, "For me, at this moment, striding away from the crowd, what has become important above all is that I should neither be contaminated by the atrocity that is about to be committed nor poison myself with impotent hatred of its perpetrators. I cannot save the prisoners, therefore let me save myself. Let it at the very least be said, if it ever comes to be said, if there is ever anyone in some remote future interested to know the way we lived, that in this farther outpost of the Empire of light there existed one man who in his heart was not a barbarian." To avoid

barbarism in his heart (inside himself), he necessaril
public (outside himself). For him to reach agreement
therefore, he needed to act politically for the town a
ity. In other words, he distinguished himself from t
because he acted upon his existential struggle, thus making it a
political one. They were unable or unwilling to respond to him, let
alone speak for themselves. Yet as long they remained banished,
ultimately so would he for lack of a public before whom he could
appear. It made no difference that he possessed the will to act. In
contrast to nonmodern polities in which banishment is an external
and unlikely sentence, Coetzee's portrait shows it as the organizing
principle of the sovereign state's interior space. One need not be
banned from that space, because everyone is a priori banned in it.

FROM MONADS TO NOMADS

The harrowing upshot is that migrant-hood stands at the core of
modern political, economic, and social life. The atomizing effects
that generate migrant-hood firstly convert living people into isolated monads and secondly jumpstart monads into circulating
nomads (leaving this a disempowered status, as described in Part 2).
Monads are created by rendering a particular speaking subject into
an abstract, stereotyped, and voiceless object. State sovereignty is
premised on homogenizing the citizenry into a timeless, national
essence defeating the need for any particular citizen to speak. The
economy only asks that a laborer, physical or cognitive, provide
labor power in the form either of repetitive bodily movements or
of rational calculations. The capacities to perform these tasks are
incumbent in basic human physiology, which therefore require no
particular person to conduct them. Anyone can be trained, even if
some have more aptitude for particular tasks than others. Social
relations hold together precisely by discouraging direct contact
among people who can otherwise speak publicly about ethical
issues, lest they undermine economic processes over which they

hitherto lacked control. This silencing effect is tantamount to banishment as the basis of mass society. Added together, the distinction between "citizen" and "migrant" begins to evaporate if rootlessness, detachment, and marginalization are the latter's allegedly definitive characteristics.

Agamben and Arendt find similar conditions underpinning the realms of politics and economy that similarly create the condition of migrant-hood. Regarding economics, Arendt explains in *The Human Condition* how the mass economy has become premised on *animal laborans*, or the laboring animal. As indicated above, this individual performs monotonous tasks that enable her only to maintain and reproduce her body and, if lucky, social position. She does not appear in the world as the particular individual that she is because the world does not need her in particular; rather, she is only needed to perform generic, repetitive tasks rendering her an abstract human who cannot be distinguished from other humans and who leaves no lasting legacy in the world. Arendt distinguishes *animal laborans* from *homo faber*, who crafted durable goods. Instead of laboring under stressful conditions, *homo faber* worked with his hands according to his own skills and creativity. He controlled the process of production, unlike *animal laborans*, and left his particular mark in the world, which lasted beyond his lifespan in the products he himself had crafted and which became part of the durable human artifice. Even today's creative industrial designer, producing signature commodities, well understands that his products are disposable in the face of decay, obsolescence, or changing fashion. One designer implied the futility when describing how he designs a chair, for example. He first asks, "How can I put my fingerprint on it, and differentiate itself [*sic*] from everybody else or every other designer in a way? And, am I playing a game to show that I can differentiate or am I actually really doing something that is contributive, because this is the big issue here with design . . . : Are the things we are doing really making an effect and making change?" Yet he later argues that no product should last, and presumably the designer's fingerprint along with it: "If the shelf life for high technology is less than eleven months, [products] should be all 100% disposable. . . . Why on earth does anything have to be built to be permanent?"

The industrial designer's predicament illustrates the reduction of *homo faber* into *animal laborans*. Ironically, while the rise of *animal laborans* deprives the particular individual of a public appearance, the mass economy depends squarely on him. For *animal laborans* functions as the basis of economic and administrative processes—and now does so at all levels of education and income. While any given individual qua *animal laborans* can be legitimately disposed of, the category itself is the foundation of the modern mass economy, ranging from the factory worker, the creative industrial designer, and the financial analyst. Each of these employees is equally prone to layoff, loss of benefits, and the degradation of utilitarianism. Hence, *animal laborans* is included as an abstract laborer, but is systematically excluded as a particular person whether in the form of *homo faber* or anyone else.

Arendt's *animal laborans* corresponds to Agamben's *homo sacer* (sacred man) on whom the modern nation-state is built. More specifically, Agamben reasons that the essential characteristic of *homo sacer* is that he may be killed without punishment for the killer, but he may not be ritually sacrificed. So, on the one hand, *homo sacer* is such a dispensable character that his death merits no ceremonial honors, as these would symbolically acknowledge his personhood as a constituent part of the cosmological order (thus, the importance of Hektor's funeral ceremony). On the other, *homo sacer* cannot be categorically disposed of because sociopolitical order is premised upon this generic individual. The modern sovereign nation-state then is built upon *homo sacer* so that it can materialize only through the inclusion of the same category of people (national citizens) whom it systematically excludes as particular individuals. Individual particularity must be eradicated, or to put it more subtly, individual particularity cannot be given a political presence lest mass sovereignty evaporate as people constitute a polity of their own, that is, a direct democracy composed of particular speaking subjects. Marx himself recognizes the tight link between the rise of mass democracy and the laboring class when he writes early on in *Capital* that human labor could not obtain its abstract, commodified form "until the concept of human equality had already acquired the permanence of a fixed popular opinion." If all laborers and all citizens are equal (the same), then they are also exchangeable, interchangeable, and dispensable. Or as Agamben wryly notes, "If today there is no longer any one clear figure of the sacred man, it is perhaps because we are all virtually *homines sacri.*"

The amalgamation of people into a mass equalizes them on the basis of alleged essential qualities that renders any apparent differences as trivial or derivative. Indeed, this radical equalization, so central to Enlightenment thought, nevertheless presages the destruction of individual particularity as the basis of politics, or rather, there is no longer a need for politics in any constructive sense of the term. Politics gets reduced to the economics of administration and to the administration of the economy, replete with circulating bodies (whether commanded or self-governing). Democracy gets reduced to technocracy. After working hours, withdrawal from society now seems like an enticing prospect because society has no place for the individual as such. Indeed, the appeal of contemporary liberalism is precisely that it asks that the individual be left alone. That appeal's negative permutations appear in the metaphor of the living dead that we see, for example, in Tocqueville's political theory describing democracy as a collection of men living lives worse than death; in the notion of social death as a shared characteristic of slaves and laborers tied to the repetition of biological time; and even in the widespread interest in popular culture in zombies and vampires living both within and on the edge of mainstream society.

These conditions, of course, do not mean that individuals see themselves as zombies, abstractions, or atomized workers, but only that atomization greatly conditions our interactions with others. Furthermore, it does not mean that acts of resistance, solidarity movements, and NGOs operating in civil society (a problematic term) do not provide important countermeasures, but rather that these are an uphill struggle by design, with low chances of long-term success. They might succeed in ameliorating society's most alienating effects, but too often their livelihood depends on funding sources that preclude an approach to politics organized on a radically different basis. As Žižek puts it, these efforts must accept "the present liberal parliamentary consensus . . . which precludes any serious questioning of how this liberal-democratic order is complicitous in the phenomena it officially condemns and, of course, any serious attempt to imagine a society whose socio-political order would be different."

The strange situation thus arises in which people do not live in a *polity* (a term that sounds naïvely quaint to modern ears) governed through the deliberations between particular people, but rather in a *society* in which government should create the conditions so that one can maximize private interests. Yet, to be *deprived* of a polity is to be condemned to a life *in private*, consumed by private interests. This deprivation might sound like salvation. Our strong liberal sentiments have us striving for the freedom of privacy, an inclination that increasing state surveillance has intensified. However, this valid concern misses the deeper point about deprivation in mass society: the migrant whom we condescendingly pity for his displacement from home becomes no more or less displaced than the citizen who might not have moved a block from where she was born. The deprivation of publicly constituted space results in the systematic detachment of particular people from each other, leaving everyone to live their lives in private, as unmoored migrants. The modern evaporation of the public has been the godsend of neoliberalism precisely because it permits clever individuals with adequate resources to flourish in private (or privatized) activity. But this situation isolates and deprives the well-resourced individual as well as the needy one. The former's greater material security, access to commodified pleasurable experiences, and even influence in party politics does not erase this point. These assets do not grant the wealthy a jointly constituted public space, but only the opportunity to reproduce structures of inequality in their own favor and, in the process, to isolate themselves in gated communities and luxury resorts.

However, we need to understand more than just how people are atomized. Despite atomization, or perhaps because of it, we feel an imperative, coming from nowhere in particular, that we must keep busy. Idleness is the bane of the middle class because idle people neither produce nor consume. Most dangerously, they might discuss the conditions of their existence, or at least ironize it with a sardonic wit that once flourished in socialist Europe, where economic inefficiency was taken for granted. To preclude the critical thinking afforded by idle time, the prized virtue of neoliberalism has become *busyness*, which transforms a society of atomized monads into a sea of ever-circulating nomads remaining politically disempowered. These nomads' frenetic activity (discussed in Part 2) is easily mistaken for original action (discussed in Part 3). To obscure the difference is to obscure the site of sovereign struggle.

PART 2 **ACTIVITY: ATOMIZATION THROUGH CONNECTION**

Let us not waste our time in idle discourse! (*Pause. Vehemently.*) Let us do something, while we have the chance! It is not every day that we are needed. Not indeed that we personally are needed. Others would meet the case equally well, if not better.

—Samuel Beckett, *Waiting for Godot*

The framing of idleness as a personal flaw works well for neoliberal logic because the free time that it would offer would risk people thinking about and discussing the absence of politics and the presence of migrant-hood. The commonly accepted antidote to this atomization is to get "connected." We are encouraged to do so at every turn for the sake of our social lives as well as our professional ones. We must network, develop savvy social skills, and become engaged in what people are doing. On the surface, it is not migrant-hood that conditions the contemporary world, but rather the very opposite: connectedness. Yet it is curious that we should need constant reminders to establish connections if they really are so commonplace. In the form of direct reciprocities, connections were the threads that wove together societies of all types prior to modernity and in present-day spaces where people are not fully incorporated into it. One could not have imagined life without connections in so-called primitive societies, classical states, or feudal systems. To stress their importance would have been to stress the obvious, much like reminding someone that air is necessary for the sake of breathing. Today, the challenge is not simply imagining a world with connections, but rather imagining a world in which the term carries substantial meaning with respect to political action.

"Connections" have come to serve the neoliberal priority of productive economic behavior through project cooperation (quite literally, *co*-operation in a process). Historically, the term signified bonds between objects, not people. Drawing from the Latin *conectere* (to join or fasten together with), it appeared in the Renaissance lexicon as a technological term meaning to bind together physical elements. The word "connective" began by 1839 to modify the biological term "tissue," which brought it to the realm of the biologically functioning human, but not to people as joint political actors endowed with the power of initiative. In 1881, it appeared in French as *connecter*, meaning to "establish a relationship with." By 1926, it applied to getting in touch with someone via telephone, and by 1942 it meant to "awaken meaningful emotions, establish rapport."[1] At that point, we became linguistically oriented to conceive of our social lives as dependent upon technologically mediated communication. Yet it is difficult to conclude that connections in this regard either result in people's political empowerment or mitigate the structural conditions of their migrant-hood. Instead, this type of connection keeps us busy. It is the *busyness* of the neoliberal individual that precludes his using connections to constitute polities, that is, durable agreements for coexistence based on particular people's own assessments of how to live in the world. We become economically and administratively engaged, while remaining politically atomized.

---

1. The Online Etymological Dictionary. http://www.etymonline.com/index.php?search=connect

Part 2 unpacks how the trick of simultaneously atomizing and connecting people is achieved. Exposing this trick reveals how the condition of migrant-hood renders us both lonely and active, two adjectives that can apply equally to the migrant and the citizen. This trick requires privileging the mind's faculty of cognition over its faculty of thinking. In so doing, it marks out the threshold between cognition and thinking as the site of the struggle between transcendent sovereign power and the particular spaces of appearance, respectively. The organization of capital accumulation then coordinates our brains, in the form of cognitive power (through information technology systems), and our bodies, in the form of manual labor power (through the logistics of production), in order to channel both powers into endless cycles of production, consumption, and administration. The precondition of this massive integration of human energy is to reduce human plurality to its shared, generic, animal capacities. To be sure, the capacity to labor physically and calculate rationally does not distinguish the human from the animal. This situation obstructs people's ability to organize politically because it does not tolerate particular perspectives unless they advance economic and administrative processes themselves. Creativity and particularity become nothing more than a means by which one gains a comparative advantage in the marketplace or identifies another niche to sell another product or service. If action is the struggle we initiate to constitute our world differently because we determine it is unjust in its present condition, then activity is the effort we undertake for the sake of the activity itself and nothing more. In a neoliberal context, activity achieves not merely the maintenance of the status quo, but its proliferation across space and into the deep recesses of our psychic lives.

THINKING VERSUS COGNITION; OR, THE HOWS AND WHYS OF BUILDING CONNECTIONS

The subjects of contemporary liberal society are caught in a bind. On the one hand, they must be isolated from other people lest together they constitute their own sovereign polity on their own negotiated terms. On the other, they must be "connected" to exponentially enhance a liberal, capitalist economy that by design must not slow down or contract. The very atomization of mass society described in Part 1 brings forward the generic person capable of doing this work. Now isolated, this person can be connected to, and readily disconnected from, others insofar as they work together on a "process" that under their own volition might obstruct, redirect, redefine, dismantle, or recreate in a radically different form.

For the sake of activity itself (not action), individual agency must be contained and delimited. It must activate the individual's creative capacities to solve technical problems and to seek new areas of expansion, while discouraging ethical reflections about their activities' effects on the surrounding world. In so doing, the question "how" must take precedence over the question "why"— "How can we do this task?" rather than "Why should we do this task?" "How" asks a technical question, while "why" asks an ethical question. The former serves economy and administration, while the latter leads to politics; we are routinely invited to ask the question "how" as it leads to improved efficiency in a given process, or to discover new areas where its template can be applied. In contrast, the question "why" destabilizes the process and is regularly discouraged. It can radically upset the very basis of how people are organized. The answers to "how" absorb and domesticate the unlimited supply of human ingenuity. The "how" question shows no concern per se with ethics, because its inherent utilitarianism focuses on the means rather than the ends or purpose of the activity. As such, the political subject (which asks "why") is denied appearance, but the generic laboring subject (which asks "how") is welcomed into the fold. This situation leads to a vicious circle in which the ends get dissolved into the means, rendering the purpose of the activity nothing more than the activity itself. No nobler or more meaningful goal is at stake other than the stability

of the "system" and the "health" of the economy (as if the economy were the living organism rather than the living people tied
into it). The ultimate cost of privileging "how" over "why" is the
reduction of the speaking subject to an object (even if it is a creative one) that efficiently serves the template at work. Each individual necessarily contains both questioning subjects—asking how
and why—inside the self; the denial of persons qua political subjects begins by refusing to invite them into a conversation about
the *meaning*, the why, of what they are doing in conjunction with
others. This gross imbalance between "how" and "why" surely has
much to do with the anti-intellectual character of middle-class
society, which values productivity, efficiency, and convenience
above all else.

The political importance of the why/how distinction is found in
Arendt's reworking of Kant's *Critique of Judgment*, which she
described as the political philosophy he meant to write and among
the most original aspects of his work. The significance of her interpretation is that she saw in *Critique of Judgment*, and in contrast to
his *Critique of Practical Reason*, an understanding of the political that
did not rely on universally applicable truths. As such, it suggests a
politics that does not require transcendent forms of sovereignty or
abstract political agents such as "people," "class," or "nation," but
only particular people bound by their own lived experiences. To her
mind, this possibility offered a new understanding of politics that
had not been fully grasped in formal political philosophy from Plato
to Marx, the latter whom she saw as the last philosopher of the Western tradition, and moreover that Nietzsche and Heidegger could not
fully articulate.

Through Kant's *Critique of Judgment*, Arendt examines two of
the mind's faculties: the faculty of thinking, which would correspond to the question "why," and the faculty of cognition, which
would correspond to the question "how." The faculty of cognition
seeks logical certainty about what is given to the senses. The faculty of thinking searches for meaning in ambiguous circumstances

through speculation. Both faculties are stimulated by the external world, but each orients us to it in significantly different ways. Cognition seeks to impose order *upon* the world by aligning it with logics that hold together in the abstract. Thinking seeks to ethically orient the thinker *in* the world by considering the alternative perspectives that the thinker encounters in other persons and situations. Cognition must see the empirical world as objects, not subjects, because when imposing abstract logic it cannot accommodate alternative standpoints, even though it can appropriate them. More accurately, it cannot establish a relationship of equality with any subject it encounters because that would grant the particular subject an equal voice in the matter at hand and risk an unpredictable outcome. That situation would transform a voiceless object to be acted upon (or at least conditioned to act within certain parameters) into a speaking subject, which would put the given process at risk since no two subjects would share completely identical perspectives on that process. If all subjects had voice, then the basis of their interaction (their government, as it were) could not be found in abstract logic but rather in unpredictable negotiated agreements among people shaped by their different lived experiences. Thinking, therefore, is required to do this work because it is capable of representing another person's perspective in the thinker's mind when she is deciding on an ethical course of action. Thinking enhances imagination because the mind accumulates images of alternative perspectives with which new directions can be conceived. Thinking does not involve naïve empathy with others, but nevertheless it "is possible only where the standpoint of all others are open to inspection."

Economy and administration, seeking efficient population management, prefer cognition over thinking because cognition strives for the certainty of the status quo rather than questions it. This situation pushes aside the faculty of thinking, thus precluding the technocrat's consideration of other individuals' standpoints and encouraging policy indifference toward them. Thinking, unlike cognition, threatens the order of mass society in two ways: first, it removes the thinker from the world, because thinking requires solitude during which she is not doing her part to prop that world up; and second, it presages alternative courses of action based on the thinker's assessment of other people's standpoints that she has encountered in the world. Thinking is the two-in-one dialogue between her and herself in which both sides must reach an inner agreement before she can be at peace with herself. What prompts her to think and ultimately act are injustices for which she will not bear responsibility by passively reproducing the world that enables them. Otherwise, she will have to live with herself as an unjust person because she sees herself as an agent of those injustices until she acts to rectify them. As thinkers, therefore, we do not return to the world as the same person we were before, because we have now reassessed our relation to it by examining those alternative standpoints.

Thinking, rather than cognition, precedes human connections if those connections are political. If we have decided that a new course of action is appropriate, then we have made an ethical judgment. This judgment is the basis of joint political action when we persuade (or become persuaded by) others to move in a new direction. Thinking and judging (along with willing and acting) are thus the basis of politics understood as a positive endeavor. Thinking is not an isolated activity, as we might be romantically inclined to portray it. Although thinking occurs in solitude, this solitude is necessary so that the individual can try to reconcile himself to the surrounding world: first by assessing an unprecedented situation, then by returning to a public space to persuade others of the merits of his ideas for dealing with it. In that public encounter the particular individual's wholeness and integrity are obtained because others acknowledge the validity of his existence by considering his perspective on an equal basis as their own. Since each person in this public encounter is considering the others in the same way, political *being* is established "inter-subjectively," meaning that we obtain a worldly reality as our particular selves in the very act of constituting public space between us. "Connections" begin to obtain substantial meaning in this regard. Politics must be about *meaning* rather than pure reason if it is going to bring particular individuals to life.

However, the connections that neoliberalism encourages us to form through cooperation are based on our cognitive skills, not our capacity as thinking beings. This situation does not require the full person. By virtue of having a mind each person can deploy cognitive skills equally well if given adequate training or experience. Cognition works the same in each person and so it does not distinguish one person from another. Through logical reasoning, we can determine the most efficient means to an end, just as a bird (like any other bird) can determine how far it can risk flying to obtain food while leaving the nest exposed to predators. In contrast, no two people *think* alike because no two people have lived the same life course; thinking is inseparable from the particular experiences of the thinker. Two people's perspectives will never mirror each other completely. Thus, what they think—the way they will ethically assess a given situation—will differ, or at least cannot be guaranteed to be the same. Cognition does not ask us to reassess on the basis of hearing other people's standpoints; it does not ask us to recognize other people as worth hearing in any serious way. In this context, thinking is relegated to the margins and even mocked when brave souls try to bring what they think to public light: "You think too much." "Yes, but can you solve a real problem?" "You are pretentious." "You are an elitist." Or even, "What can you do with a liberal arts degree, anyway?" (Coetzee's magistrate even endured torture.) The individual, therefore, is not "connected" in an open-ended discussion with different people about the meaning of their activity. Instead, she will be connected only in order to advance processes that are evaluated on their economic efficiency alone. Here the word "connections" takes on a sinister meaning. To connect people to economic and administrative practices on the basis of their cognitive or manual labor power is to connect them in their animal capacities only. These connections are not the basis of political action, but rather manifestations of the condition of migrant-hood.

SYSTEMS AND THE GENERIC PERSON(ALITY)

While much has been written regarding the atomization and animalization of humans through industrial labor, the point holds equally well for cognitive labor. Connecting people through their faculty of cognition achieves the same effect and arguably penetrates ever further into the fabric of daily life. The U.S. government's recent plan to reduce office space at the General Services Administration (GSA) illustrates how connections operate as both a cause and an effect of atomization. Prompted by Congress's Telework Enhancement Act, GSA hopes to usher in a new corporate model for the federal government that would save $24 million in rent plus further savings on office furniture and maintenance costs and enhance overall "work/life balance."[2] The plan's tacit objective is to remove the employee from the workplace. GSA's reduced office space still accommodates those needing to meet in person but otherwise encourages them to connect with coworkers from elsewhere via Google Talk, e-mail, internet calling, and instant messaging.[3] After the renovation of headquarters, located one block from the White House, employees have access to less than half of the workspace than before. Their badges transmit asignal at the building entrance's turnstile to record their presence on the premises. They meet in "teaming rooms" where they log in electronically

---

2. http://www.telework.gov/telework_enhancement_act/; accessed April 3, 2014.

3. Lisa Rein, "The Federal Office Space of the Future? GSA's New Floor Plan Eschews Desk-Jockey Culture," July 15, 2013. http://www.washingtonpost.com/politics/the-federal-office-space-of-the-future-gsas-new-floor-plan-eschews-desk-jockey-culture/2013/07/15/f7e4f8dc-e975-11e2-8f22-de4bd2a2bd39_story.html; accessed July 17, 2013.

through a "room wizard." The word "teaming" is a gerund locked in a weirdly indefinite present tense: it is an activity conducted by people who have no shared past and are planning for no shared future. (No less weirdly, "teaming" compares to torture and banishment, which as mentioned holds the individual in a suspended present between life and death.) Employees merely assemble and disassemble according to the project schedule. In the form of a noun, "team" is a discernible, complete, and durable entity sharing a past, capable of constituting its own present, and able to move into an unpredictable future. The GSA neither can afford nor desires to have a "team" in its midst, but rather needs a supply of employees who are capable of "teaming," now understood as one professional skill among others, such as an ability to use to Excel or work under tight deadlines.

These individuals are known as "mobile workers" according to Agilquest, the company that installed the information technology systems that logistically manage the "mobile environment." (Again, migrant-hood is not primarily defined by the movement of people but, in this case, by their relationship to the ever-shifting terrain of digital reality.) Mobile workers must depart the teaming rooms without leaving a trace of their presence. They must keep noise and particular smells, such as their lunch or perfume, to a minimum. Walls have been removed and replaced with rolling filing cabinets that also function as seats. Whiteboards and lockers for holding purses and lunches have replaced printers and shredders. Mobile workers must reserve desks, work stations, and conference rooms in a practice called "hoteling," the term itself institutionalizing impermanence throughout the workforce. The logic behind this generically designed space assumes that one's presence is fleeting at best. In this vein, even the liberal periodical *The Economist* fears the redundancies that increased computerization will unleash on the white-collar workforce in the coming decades. But redundancies can only occur when people are reduced to their redundant, animal functions, be they the cognitive skills of the white-collar laborer or the manual skills of the blue-collar laborer. By dispensing with what makes each person unique, their co-presence poses no political threat and prepares them for having their generic skills absorbed into information technology systems. As information technology improves, no compelling reason can be found to even bring them into a shared space. These systems hold together the GSA's 3300 dispersed white-collar laborers, store the fruits of their labor, and make them immediately accessible to whoever needs them, wherever they happen to be. This system for organizing cognitive labor power could not thrive if it depended on people qua particular subjects who played a defining role in how it works and the purposes it serves. Generic laborers instead can be exchanged or replaced, and are valued for technical savvy rather than ethical judgment. The ease of connection equally facilitates disconnection.

Even the most innovative technology firms reinforce atomization through connection in their forward-thinking practices that promote health, collaboration, and creativity. They have redesigned their office space so that employees can brainstorm in groups or withdraw to a single office, depending on what needs to be done. Microsoft research buildings, such as "Building 99," put cafes on the first floor so ideas can be discussed in a relaxed, casual atmosphere. Soundproof rooms are available if one desires solitude. Other corporate campuses encourage walking-meetings on nature trails landscaped around the buildings themselves. Indeed, the health of the cognitive laborer is increasingly valued as it keeps the mind functioning and productive. Similarly, standing desks and chairs avoid the ergonomic perils of sitting too much. "Sitting is the new smoking," remarked one expert in workplace design. Corporate gyms provide treadmills with computers that allow the employee to check e-mail while exercising. Charlie Chaplin, of course, presaged the use of technology to combine health and labor into the same activity when the Little Tramp's factory boss tested an automatic eating machine on him in the 1936 film *Modern Times*. The machine automatically inserted food into the worker's mouth during the lunch hour so that his hands, located below the tray, could continue to screw rivets on the assembly line. Chaplin's parody spotlighted the absurdity of this now mainstream idea, which finely integrates the body's own metabolism into the schedule of the production cycle itself. Yet this phenomenon appeared at the beginning of industrialization and simply becomes more refined and pervasive as the decades go on.

Similarly, the contemporary conditions of cognitive laboring draw people's analytical powers into the service of national-cum-global security with ease and comfort. A new collaborative study between the U.S. intelligence community and the Good Judgment Project illustrates the point.[44] As many as three thousand people living across the United States have signed up to participate in a study to determine how well the average of their numeric responses to questions about current world events can predict those events' eventual outcome. The project was inspired by the statistically observable phenomenon that most people do poorly at solving numerical problems (for example, guessing the weight of an ox), but when a group's total number of individual guesses is averaged, the result almost exactly matches the correct answer. The collaborative study confronts not a static problem but rather a dynamic one, that is, not the weight of an ox but, the likelihood that a given security threat will emerge in the future. This is a question of probability.

Without leaving the comfort of home, participants receive basic training in probabilities. They are then given access to a secure website with carefully worded questions and with a place to enter the numerical estimate of the event's likelihood. For example, would the government of Syria announce a ceasefire agreement? Would North Korea launch a new multistage missile by the tenth of May 2014? Or would Russian armed forces enter Kharkiv

---

4. "So You Think You're Smarter than a CIA Agent," NPR broadcast, April 2, 2014. http://www.npr.org/templates/transcript/transcript.php?storyId=297839429; accessed April 11, 2014.

by the tenth of May? One participant, an elderly female pharmacist from suburban Maryland, has proved particularly good at this task even though she is not particularly strong in math. She simply finds information about the questions through Google searches, but the accuracy of her forecasts has earned her the title "superforecaster" by psychologists who study "expert judgment." She is on a team with thirty other standouts whose predictions are reportedly thirty percent better than intelligence officers with access to classified information. The woman explained, "the first two years I did this, all you do is choose numbers. You don't have to say anything about your numbers. You just choose numbers and then you see how your numbers work."

This mode of cognitive labor exemplifies how an information-processing apparatus—a flexible, innovative, and proliferating infrastructure—can penetrate into scattered areas of a country to simultaneously integrate the cognitive labor power of scattered people and obstruct direct discussions among those people about how the world *should* be organized. It thus denies their faculty of thinking altogether by precluding direct engagement with each other and with a wider plurality of speaking subjects in the world "out there." It thus reinforces atomization, not simply because it keeps the forecasters geographically isolated but because it asks them only to share cognitive assessments not ethical judgments. If three thousand random people are capable of conducting the work of forecasting for the largest military-intelligence apparatus ever known, then surely this illustrates Beckett's point quoted in the epigraph: "Not indeed that we personally are needed. Others would meet the case equally well, if not better." Yet this situation is more significant than the atomization of single persons. It suggests that the apparatus's ceaseless activities are controlled by no one in particular as the end game is the reproduction of a status quo that depends upon abstract citizen-laborers but denies their appearance as particular speaking subjects. The counterargument that the status quo would be much worse without this intelligence apparatus would at best only address the question of liberation, not freedom. If correct, then this apparatus enables lives to be lived more securely, but security, as an end in itself, does not beget freedom.

These different laboring conditions (at the GSA, at the campuses of high-tech corporations, or at the homes of the CIA's superforecasters) eliminate the human factor altogether if the term "human" connotes the particular person rather than a generic laborer. Indeed, it is not the person qua thinking subject that is connected but rather the individual qua cognitive laborer. That individual is rendered compatible with a computer. This situation allows the employee to be removed from the company of coworkers; to be rendered interchangeable with other employees; and to be exchanged for or integrated into an algorithmic program. Often the employee is only grudgingly seen, not to be remembered or perhaps even recalled after departing—hence the GSA's moratorium on lasting smells. The interchangeability of employees prized for their "teaming" capabilities means that employees as particular speaking subjects cannot create a shared past with others that they themselves define. Thus, they cannot constitute their work space as their own place. To assemble people without pasts—or to deny their pasts—is to create what Eric Wolf called "people without history," even if he wrote about the world's colonized, enslaved, and manual laborers in global capitalism's earlier phases. In so doing, peoples and cultures become timeless objects (his metaphor was billiard balls), thus concealing the field of power relations from which those objects were abstracted. Rendered an object, and so removed of voice, they are there to be managed, put to work, or disposed of, depending on the moment's prevailing needs.

This process of objectification can occur rather willingly, as it reaches down into the construction of ourselves as people who can "fit in" at the workplace: generic requirements for work evoke generic presentations of self. The successful cognitive laborer internalizes—or at least learns to present himself through—generic personality traits that are often formally cultivated through career counseling, professional workshops, and lifestyle advertising targeted at his demographic. *The Economist* reports that forty percent of the heads of FTSE 100 companies rely on "personal coaches," and that one of the most popular courses at Harvard Business School examines how to guard against an obsession with short-term success. The coaches and courses function to keep egocentric CEOs in line with the demands of stockholders. They introduce a social conservatism that stabilizes interaction among otherwise diverse and particular people by encouraging them to act in safe and recognizable ways. Communication—and our chances of earning a wage—improves when everyone knows what to expect from people they have never met and will not see after the project's completion.

The origins of generic personality reach back to the eighteenth century with the rise of politeness and middle-class manners. In the United Kingdom, for example, it corresponds to the rise of commercial society and the breaking down of caste-based society. This economic change likewise liberated many people from confining kinship and village networks by sending them into the marketplace to earn profit. People had to learn to interact with those who were not historically of their station and who had no place in their traditional cosmology. This shift required a code of conduct that any particular person could master and then use as a guide to interact with others on a utilitarian basis. It particularly appealed to the upwardly mobile and it homogenized speech patterns between genders and between ranks. The new politeness insisted, as it still does, that the speaker not suggest that he knows too much, but just enough to indicate an awareness of culture and serious topics. Conversation was to be light and easy. Interlocutors could mock each other, but only in innocuous ways. One should demonstrate moral sentiment but avoid an air of theological command. The cumulative effect was to produce a society of safely similar people whose equality was achieved through weeding out differences. In parallel, the working class, on whom politeness was not immediately impressed, was also liberated, so to speak, as "free laborers." These were former peasants enclosed out of agricultural lands, who now needed to travel to towns and cities to work in the new manufacturing centers and ultimately in the factories of the industrial revolution. As the economic conditions of migrant-hood began to solidify, it started to release people from traditional social bonds, to standardize codes of conduct, and to circulate people according to the spatial requirements of commerce and production. This situation formed the terrain for monadic nomads (or "domestic migrants" in today's technical parlance), who were deemed interchangeable, exchangeable, and dispensable.

However, a world that depends fundamentally on information technology and generic codes of conduct to structure its commu-nication is not a political world but rather a technocratic one that encourages us to come forward as nonpersons. Such an apparatus prevents particular people from mutually constituting worlds while it continuously integrates them as economic animals into processes of securing, producing, and consuming. One must fit the social expectations that underpin an apparatus's technical requirements or be left to fend for oneself. Thus, while the prolif-eration of information technology has facilitated our ability to communicate, we should be wary of how this development is pre-sented as a social advancement. It falsely implies that communica-tion was lacking in the past, and that it overcomes atomization rather than induces it. Moreover, it confuses communication, which is the mere exchange of information, with deliberation, which is a negotiation through which people establish as equals the terms of their coexistence.

An eerie comparison emerges regarding, technology, video screens, and social relations. Orwell famously illustrated the screen's power in isolating us to generate mass conformity. Big Brother's haunting face peered at the citizens of Oceania in nearly every location. Fear kept people alone and in line. Strangely, in neoliberal society we likewise have ubiquitous contact with screens, which induce conformity through the excitement and pleasure of their titillating graphics rather than through someone's terrorizing gaze. These screens too keep us in line by keeping us engaged in cooperative, productive activity and by demonstrating to those to whom we are connected that we are safely normal, even if in our own quirky ways (via Facebook, for example, where we can list our particular tastes in music, films, and other leisurely activities). Yet we are still alone. We become passive and active simultaneously, but still refrain from action. T. S. Eliot's remark about the television fifty years ago has retained its pertinence in today's more refined era of digital communication: "It is a medium of entertainment which permits millions of people to listen to the same joke at the same time, and yet remain lonesome."

THE SITE OF THE STRUGGLE

To make this situation even more slippery, recall from above how the new workplace boasts of many features that are similar to those in our understanding of positive politics: deeply horizontal relations, the reliance on the particular person's initiative, and a willingness to let people organize in ways suitable to themselves. To this list we can add, with Hardt and Negri, a celebration of difference, the importance of free play, and the overall breaking down of old boundaries. Those who used to be excluded have become the celebrated agents of production and consumption. This unique individual is prioritized over the generic mass. The new bosses in this arrangement are in charge of "diversity management" so that the creative energies of different people can be drawn into the equally diverse methods of profit maximization, and all for the sake of making the world a better place. At the same time, Hardt and Negri see the varied modes in which contemporary capital organizes labor as the same modes through which the multitude can resist capital, synopsized in *Empire*'s epigraph quoting Ani DiFranco: "Every tool is a weapon if you hold it right." Before such resistance occurs, however, we should specify how politics is obstructed. With fuzzy glasses it can be difficult to distinguish between the *activities* of neoliberalism's laborers and the *actions* of those seeking changes at a foundational level. The difference is whether the people in question can, and do, deliberate on the question "why" as a prelude to action. The neoliberal workplace invites only one's faculty of cognition (welcoming the question, "How can we improve the efficiency of our performance?"), whereas those open to foundational change invite the faculty of thinking ("Why should we do things for this purpose rather than another?"). *Activity*, for its suppression of the faculty of thinking, denies the particular subject and so renders her atomized and politically inert. The basis of the given activity cannot be touched. For this reason, the site of the struggle between a politics of appearance and a political-economic state premised on transcendental forms is the boundary between cognition and thinking (and so between how and why; activity and action; generic object and the particular speaking subject; and animal and human). I suggest that this proximity facilitates Empire's appropriation of the multitude's creative potential per Hardt and Negri's formulation.

Enron's advertising campaign "Ask Why" illustrates the easy slippage from thinking to cognition (and so from action to activity). One commercial dedicates thirty seconds to explaining the word "why" and praising those who have asked it for making the world a better place. This commercial bravely asserts that "why" is an "abrupt word" and the "chosen word of the nonconformist" (a scene flashes of a worker getting clubbed over the head by a capitalist), the "defiant" (flash to a statue of Gandhi), and the "visionary" (flash to Abraham Lincoln). It is, furthermore, "a confrontational word." To signify its potential to inaugurate new beginnings the narrator explains that "it challenges what's thought to be impossible . . . if you are not afraid to ask why, you can change whatever it is you want." The commercial ends with a note that *Fortune* magazine identified Enron as the "most innovative company in America." Lest we think that such corporate entities standing at the vanguard of capital accumulation also stand at the vanguard of freedom, we simply need to recognize that Enron's mobilization of the question "why"—as in "why" are we not charging customers for bandwidth? or "why" are we avoiding exploring new markets?—is done in the service of the question "how." "Why" is applied only to improve the means to the end of profit maximization, which is nothing more than a means to further accumulation of capital. There is no striving for a stable and meaningful world. It is directed only at the efficiency of practice for practice's sake, rather than practice's ethical basis. The faculty of thinking was never invited into the corporate boardroom because the effects of Enron's economic activity on other people was never considered. This modus operandi cheapens the question "why." Had anyone at Enron genuinely asked "why"—and if any thoughtful individual on the inside could have risked uttering it— then many people's livelihoods might have remained intact.

Similarly, this close proximity has also cheapened the term *judgment*. We frequently hear this term in tacit association with cognitive activity: given the circumstances, what is the likelihood of a favorable outcome? The cognitive laborer's judgments would offer a cost-benefit assessment and an "action" plan written from the employer's standpoint. Here the demonstration of good judgment lies in how well the plan's objectives are met or, in the case of the Good Judgment Project and CIA forecasting, how closely the prediction corresponded to how events actually transpired. However, this laboring activity did not consider the perspective of any other person tied to the circumstances under consideration, meaning it did not decide on a plan of action in equal dialogue with others. The forecaster assessed objects in motion—as a meteorologist would assess air pressure, humidity, and wind speed to predict the weather—not subjects immersed in power relations. Judgment here does not pertain to ethics or politics, and so it has nothing to do with *thinking*. To endow this cognitive activity with the description of "good judgment" is to cynically turn a blind eye to ethics. In contrast, if *thinking* were invited into the process, then the perspectives of people tied to the circumstances would have been the first consideration and the resulting judgment would have been an ethical one.

THE POLITICAL PERIL OF LONELINESS WITHIN THREE IDEOLOGIES

Intellectuals of different persuasions have long identified isolation, loneliness, and political disempowerment as interrelated features of mass society, whether these appear in totalitarianism, fascism, or liberal democracy. A comparison of how these three elements do their work in each of these respective ideologies sheds light on how neoliberalism utilizes them to achieve atomization through connection. People remain unable to form political connections in neoliberalism, on the basis of thinking, but are well endowed with economic connections, on the basis of cognitive assessments of possible gains. In totalitarian societies, Arendt argues that fear of state terror isolates individuals, which precludes the forming of bonds between people, bonds that are necessary to constitute public spaces. The individual remains constantly suspicious of others and so cannot form spaces of appearance in which people mutually confirm each other's particular identities through deliberations on matters of public concern. Furthermore, this atomization and suspicion deprive individuals of the opportunity to *think* about the world from the multiplicity of perspectives that one can best encounter through direct engagement with others. As a result, totalitarianism corrals atomized individuals together with an "iron band" of ideology. Ideology supplies an interpretative framework in which one can find coherence in the assorted facts found in the world without having to engage anyone or examine anything from their different positions in the world. The cognitive work of deduction becomes the means through which the world is understood. Since the individual lacks meaningful contact with other individuals, the faculty of thinking is marginalized because no other speaking subject is present to confront the individual with an alternative ethical position that prompts someone to withdraw and discuss the new encounter with one's self. For Arendt (and others such as Eric Hoffer and Eric Fromm), the lonely individual, whom mass society generates by its very modus operandi, is susceptible to ideological thinking because its purely rational line of reasoning enables the individual to comprehend the messiness of the empirical world without having to properly engage it. To be sure, totalitarianism established itself unevenly across its space of control; to varying degrees, resistance was certainly present; and ultimately people cannot be entirely made to *not* think. However, the key point is that in a totalitarian situation the pressure clearly moves toward a radical atomization that reaches a psychic level and diminishes the prospects of political action.

While Arendt was primarily concerned with the function of ideology in totalitarianism, her analyses always begin with the plight of the individual in mass society in general rather than totalitarianism in particular. Therefore, we can still direct her insights toward neoliberal ideology. While both ideologies rely heavily on cognition, the utopias that each imagines are significantly different. Communism posited an inevitable historical movement toward a worker's paradise, and fascism posited an inevitable global triumph of the Aryan race. Neoliberalism offers a belief, similarly disconnected from empirical reality, that each individual will achieve inner perfection through the activities of consumption, production, technical innovation, and continuing education (witness the enormous number of self-help books available online or in bookstores). Schematically put, while communism and fascism anticipated an externally perfect world, neoliberalism aims for internally perfect individuals. The former saw their utopia as a steady state coterminous with global space. Theoretically, all people would be content in their social roles, and the utopia itself would remain eternally the same. Yet totalitarian movements under Hitler and

Stalin featured profound antipathy toward state bureaucracies (even if these movements relied on them), because the *static* quality implied in the state concept contradicts the perpetual motion required to fulfill these respective movements' utopic goals. (Since utopias are unattainable within the confines of the actually existing world, then totalitarian movements become aspirational movements that can never stop.) Hence, the party replaced or overrode state functionaries and presented itself as the embodiment of a pregiven historical process by constantly expanding into, and profoundly transforming, ever more realms of daily life. Another eerie similarity thus appears insofar as the dream of neoliberalism is not to establish a steady state, which totalitarian movements could not attain anyway. Indeed, it has gone one step further by abandoning the pretense that such a state is even desirable. Rather, neoliberalism's dream is to create steady *individuals*, meaning people who calculate with the greatest degree of certainty possible so that they maximize their gains as they continuously and eagerly recreate the world through economic activity. The result is an ever-changing world that is intentionally under constant improvement by people who are constantly striving to improve themselves as they strive for inner utopia (likewise a goal that cannot be reached, leaving the individual caught up in constant aspirational pursuits). Despite its dynamism, this world lacks political action like its totalitarian cousin; neither exists as a stable world and both convert their inhabitants into migrants.

Foucault's read on neoliberalism helps us elucidate the social underpinnings of its dream of an inner utopia. It captures the foundational role of dissolvable connections in neoliberalism and so helps clarify why it induces migrant-hood and renders people apolitical. Foucault posits in *The Birth of Biopolitics* that two types of subjects come forward in modern liberal society: the subject of right and the subject of interest. The subject of right consists of the individual willing to give up some of his rights to the sovereign in order to retain others so that he can live peaceably in the world. This individual voluntarily enters into a social contract with the bureaucratic state to guarantee his basic existence lest the world remain in a state of nature, which threatens everyone alike. The subject of interest consists of the individual who pursues his economic interest through partnerships and associations that work to mutual advantage. The subject of interest is a discrete individual composed of irreducible choices or, rather, choices unique to that person which ultimately require no further justification. For example, I want health because illness is unpleasant; no more need be said. This development is important because it marks the first appearance of interest as "both immediately and absolutely subjective will." In contrast to the subject of right, the subject of interest evades traditional state sovereignty to pursue private interests through temporary but mutually beneficial partnerships. Those activities will transpire not through lasting connections of a political type, through mutually recognized speaking subjects, but rather through associations of interest that are designed to disassemble once the participating individuals achieve their private agendas. In contrast to the enduring social contract between the sovereign and the subject of right, the subjects of interest's bonds are designed to be broken. Foucault appropriately calls them "associations of disassociation."

These two subject positions, living within a single individual, assume two different and irreconcilable worlds. The subject of right lives in the closed, bound, and totalized world of state sovereignty. The subject of interest operates in an open-ended space, which exceeds the individual's and the sovereign's field of vision. It is, by definition, non-knowable and non-totalizable. Both the sovereign and the subject of interest are blind to the full dynamism of that field, but in any case economic rationality, the work of cognition, is the modus operandi for participating in it. Moreover, a sovereign that could establish a perfect view of this field would be an anathema to it as it would soon desire to control that field as it does its own sovereign space. Therefore, the subject of interest is constantly pushing back against the subject of right, and the sovereign state he upholds, so that new contracts can be formed specific to new interests. For this reason, Foucault argues, that neoliberalism measures the utility of the state only in terms of its effectiveness in creating the conditions for liberal economic transaction. Otherwise, the state is inherently viewed with suspicion.

Through the lens of market exchange, Karl Marx already understood the qualitative transformation of the social fabric implied in a world dominated by the subject of interest (the capitalist, in his analytical parlance). Capitalist exchange is not a direct reciprocity as in the case of bartering but, rather, indirect so that the market, transcending any particular location of exchange, determines the value of the traded commodity. The constant practice of exchange in this scenario requires money to signify value, and this allows a local economy to sufficiently globalize. Money allows the achievement of equivalency between different commodities so that they can be indirectly exchanged through cash purchase. As a result, Marx explains, "We see here, on the one hand, how the exchange of commodities breaks through all the individual and local limitations of the direct exchange of products, and develops the metabolic process of human labor. On the other hand, there develops a whole network of social connections of natural origin, entirely beyond the control of human agents." In other words, what develops is a dynamic and ultimately global field of economic activity into which human metabolism is integrated into the rhythm of the processes of production, exchange, and consumption, all of which subordinates human agents to those processes.

It follows from both Marx and Foucault that the neoliberal world is not held together in a rigid statist framework protected through a transcendent contract with an external sovereign. Rather, the state conditions the world so that the subject of interest constantly reorganizes it according to the utilitarian logic that he carries as an inherent faculty of his mind. With no transcendent domain above, neoliberalism insists that "there is no sovereign in economics." It instead constantly transforms the world through the frenetic activity of atomized, but temporarily connected, entrepreneurs deploying abstract, economic logics to maximize interests. The subject of interest, replete with his monadic-nomadic character, participates in an eternally transforming world, which can only assign him to a life of migrant-hood. The neoliberal rejection of sovereign authority positions it not only against traditional state sovereignty, but also against local and directly sovereign spaces constituted by people themselves. The latter's sovereign practices would invite the question "why" when debating how they should conduct their economic activity. This question obstructs neoliberal activity. The particular speaking subject, therefore, has been asked to sacrifice his voice by becoming either a subject of right (suppressed by the state's abstract sovereignty) or a subject of interest (which has no place in a world dominated by cognitively calculated objectives). While the subject of interest must be fashioned as a self-starting, autonomous agent, that agent must fashion himself as a tool (albeit a creative tool) driven by the utilitarian logics of production, marketing, and consumption. The result is that this autonomous agent is still reduced to an object insofar as tools are only valued to the extent they accelerate the rate of profit.

However, while a singular, absolute sovereign seems absent in a neoliberal world—and this alleged absence enables much celebratory rhetoric about freedom realized through unfettered economic activity—potential sovereign power has only subdivided into the number of particular individuals present in that world. Insofar as the faculty of cognition deals strictly with abstract, logical operations, it transcends, or endeavors to silence, the messiness of the empirical world. As such it aims to silence the particular speaking subject and the faculty of thinking along with it. The subject of interest asks that we see the world as something that can be operationalized for the sake of the operation itself. We are to produce and consume for the sake of producing and consuming so that the economy can grow for its own sake. This situation sounds remarkably similar to traditional state sovereignty, in which order in the sovereign territory is valued for nothing other than order in the sovereign territory; that is, so that it may perpetuate another day and nothing more. As Foucault explains in *Security, Territory, Population*, raison d'état refers to what is necessary to simply preserve the republic: the equilibrium between its territory, its jurisdiction, and the population. This goal is pursued on the authority of reason itself (hence raison d'état) as the mode through which that equilibrium is comprehended and maintained. Divorced from empirical reality, pure reason renders raison d'état entirely self-referential because nothing about it "refers to anything other than the state itself."

Much debate transpires about who should be resisted as the source of oppression in the so-called postmodern world: the police officer; the party official; the technical expert; the CEO? Yet the dispensability of these figures themselves indicates that the source we seek precedes even them. They themselves are subordinate to the abstract, rationalized processes they serve and thus are instruments at least as much as they are agents. As for anyone else, this point does not mean that they do not hold responsibility for their actions. Rather, it means that the logics of the system they serve are the necessary conditions of their actions, and so replacing any of these specific actors barely impacts those conditions as the ultimate source of oppression. As underwhelming as it may seem, those systemic sources might be nothing more than the hegemony of cognition over thinking, that is, abstract logics underpinning the field of oppressive human relations. These cannot be resisted at a general level. They must be exposed and situated in their particular manifestations, so that particular ways of organizing spaces of appearance in their places can be instantiated. The methods to resist that hegemony would vary according to the particulars modes in which it presents itself and according to the particular actors who initiate the action to challenge it.

The favoring of one mental faculty over another implies radically divergent political subjects, but the potential to actualize either subject resides in each human being, as we all depend on both faculties. We can use Marx's own characterization of the capitalist as one example of an agent operating with authority—but not with political being—on the basis of the faculty of cognition. He graphically describes how the capitalist's very dream destroys his political being and renders himself an agent in his own objectification as much as those whom he exploits: the capitalist is "capital personified. His soul is the soul of capital. But capital has one sole driving force, the drive to valorize itself, to create surplus-value. . . . Capital is dead labour which, vampire-like, lives only by sucking living labour, and lives the more, the more labour it sucks." The reduction of the capitalist to a vampire—not a fully live human being—occurs when cognition becomes the foundation of human relations and so enables the work of exploitation and accumulation. If the logics of capital accumulation govern the lives of the oppressor and oppressed in an economic context, then Arendt observes a similarly ghostly effect on political being in totalitarian systems governed by the logics of utilitarianism and the ideology of racial purity. She concludes, "The manipulators of this system believe in their own superfluousness as much as in that of all others, and the totalitarian murderers are all the more dangerous because they do not care if they themselves are alive or dead, if they ever lived or never were born." Thus, the oppressors themselves should oppose these systems if freedom means anything more to them than survival, while the oppressed must oppose them as a matter of survival and a precursor to freedom. Ultimately, the originating site of the struggle for freedom is located at the boundary between the faculties of cognition and thinking. Through the latter, new worlds become imaginable in which oppressed and oppressor can act as particular people rather than the instruments and objects of capitalist (re)production and totalitarianism.

It is difficult to see how political action that brings people into a public sphere as thinking and speaking subjects could emerge through the neoliberal experience. The economization of all space, privileging cognition as it does, isolates individuals and turns them into the busiest and cleverest of calculating beings. Giuseppe di Lampedusa pinpointed the pointlessness of this frenetic activity in *The Leopard* through the mouthpiece of Prince Fabrizio. This aristocrat has become an anachronism in a nationalizing Italy now dominated by an emergent bourgeoisie. Rejecting an offer to take up a seat in the new Senate, Fabrizio spells out the reason:

> I belong to an unfortunate generation, swung between the old world and the new, and I find myself ill at ease in both. And what is more, as you must have realized by now, I am without illusions; what would the Senate do with me, an inexperienced legislator who lacks the faculty of self-deception, essential requisite for wanting to guide others? We of our generation must draw aside and watch the capers and somersaults of the young around this ornate catafalque. Now you need young men, bright young men, with minds asking "how" rather than "why," and who are good at masking, at blending, I should say, their personal interests with vague public ideals.

INSUFFICIENT REASSEMBLAGE: THE POLITICALLY FLAWED BASIS OF "INTEGRATION"

A world premised on atomized but connected persons, each maximizing her position in a field of economic transaction, forces us to reconsider the meaning of "immigrant integration," a phrase that concretizes the alleged dichotomy between citizens and migrants. Integration appears as an existential "problem" based on the assumption that national society is built upon identical citizens who are all essentially the same national subject. A related assumption is that one gets acclimatized to a host society only through multiyear residency on national soil. The extended time allows the migrant to internalize the language and culture that are unique to the host nation whose citizens are themselves uniquely affiliated to their sovereign territory. The problems this situation poses for an immigrant are readily apparent. As the quintessential outsider, the migrant must make the effort to find a place in an otherwise harmonious sea of allegedly identical people.

Yet, "integration" poses problems that are of vital importance for the citizen as much as the migrant: fear of layoffs, loss of benefits, juggling multiple jobs, and the cumulative assault on one's self-esteem. Citizenship is no guarantee of employment, and employment itself is no guarantee that the laborer can provide for a family. The citizen's fluency in the national language provides an entry point into a national community through the heritage it passes on from generation to generation. Yet "national community" is also a contradiction in terms because "community" presupposes the importance of deliberations between speaking subjects, while a "nation" is composed of a mass of people numbering in the millions of whom any particular citizen only knows a handful at most. National language gets reduced to a tool that increases the citizen's chances of personal success in the national job market. These detrimental effects that citizens endure should not lead to the conclusion, much preferred by the political right, that the migrant undermines the citizen's well-being. Rather, they lead to the conclusion that mass society can easily undermine the well-being of citizens and migrants alike through systemic atomization. In effect, the term "nation" itself mystifies the absence of what it claims to present: a politics based on direct negotiations between people sharing the same space. Instead, it supports a functionalist perspective that to be a good citizen means to be nothing more than a jobholder.

Two basic questions follow: Into what is a migrant actually integrated when she is subjected to a state's integration policy? And for that matter, can we speak of citizens as integrated simply because they are citizens? Like the migrant, the citizen must primarily identify herself as either a jobholder or an aspiring jobholder. Like the migrant, the citizen is highly vulnerable to layoffs and must accept short-term contracts. Like the migrant, the citizen lacks a public in which she can appear as herself in the act of constituting a local polity. Voting rights for the citizen cannot compensate for the lack of a public space. The citizen may not feel that eerie sense of "otherness" that migrants experience in the host country, because the nationalist gaze falls upon her much less. Moreover, the citizen will not be subject to the violence of vigilante groups that harass migrants in countries around the world. This difference is not to be taken lightly. However, to entirely consign to the nationalist right the blame for migrants' marginalization would be to ignore the fact that even after (and if) the migrant receives the basic guarantee of human rights, the host country has little to offer her because it has little more to offer the citizen.

The false dichotomy between the citizen and the migrant assumed in the "integration" is implied in Foucault's analysis of the subject of interest. This subject, who lives in an ever-shifting terrain of economic activity occurring across global space, seeks no durable bonds with either citizens or migrants. The possibility of public spaces or sovereign spaces of any kind are uninteresting. The result of this ethos can only be a world of migrants. It is therefore no coincidence that neoliberals are among the most reliable supporters of pro-migrant causes because that support introduces ever more people into the economic realm. However, this act of inclusion hardly helps us push back against the general condition of migrant-hood. It only amplifies it.

POLITICS AS A NECESSARILY NEGATIVE ACT IN MASS SOCIETY

As the trick of connecting individuals through atomization works through neoliberalism's associations of disassociation, the result is a ubiquitous rootlessness matched with frenetic busyness. The point here is not whether the individual physically moves across space as does the stereotypical migrant. Rather, it is that he is structurally precluded from connecting to other people on negotiated terms to create something stable for themselves. With his usual foresight, Alexis de Tocqueville cleverly noted that in democracy "[people] form the habit of thinking of themselves in isolation and imagine that their whole destiny is in their own hands." Instead, however, "Each man is forever thrown back on himself alone, and there is danger that he may be shut up in the solitude of his own heart." The danger does not end with isolation, for it encourages despotism, which "sees the isolation of men as the best guarantee of its own permanence." Tocqueville's despotism applied to a tyranny of the majority and to that of a singular figure. It follows that a flourishing capitalist economy can appear in a liberal democracy as well as in autocratic regimes. To be sure, private interest often depends on the latter, as Žižek argues with respect to Chile, South Korea, and China in his historical analysis of the frequent failure of democratic revolutions. The belief that one's economic destiny renders him a free political subject makes the condition of migrant-hood in liberal society seem like an elevated existence. Instead, migrant-hood results in the subject's reduction to an economic animal capable of economic productivity, skilled in cognitive mental activity, but void of political appearance. Over the long term, the genius of liberalism is that it has been able to improve the material lives of millions without empowering them politically. This does not deny the fact that some people (and a precious few they are) hold great leverage over many others through their ability to reproduce structures of inequality. It means that this minority can also be rendered *homo sacer* even if their personal resources give them a better chance of surviving the status. The insight of the *homo sacer* and *animal laborans* concepts is not that people are necessarily deprived of comfortable lives. Rather, it is that people, regardless of their level of material comfort, are not empowered to constitute their own sovereign spaces if that means to govern directly and equally in deliberations with peers. And so all remain exposed to the brutality of objectification.

Political action in mass society has thus become equated with negative, though necessary acts taken against the system in the form of protest or resistance. The necessity of these measures highlights the fundamental exclusion of people from politics, not just their dissatisfaction with a policy or a law. Again, the line of communication from the individual to established power in mass society—be it legislative, executive, or corporate authority—occurs indirectly through opinion polling, voting, and surveying. These channels give voice to people only as token representatives of demographic categories. All citizens may be equal in this arrangement but they are also equally disempowered. The citizen's choices for politicians are regulated through the machinations of party politics. The party amalgamates citizens into various demographic groups, develops platforms, makes concessions, and offers incentives to them based on careful calculations. Direct political participation in mass democracy, beyond protest or resistance, is limited to zones that people must carve out despite the larger regulatory contexts in which they operate. When public policy or law becomes unbearable, citizens can of course complain to the relevant bureaucrat or lawmaker. Failing that, protests can be organized, which may well succeed in changing the policy or law. The system may accommodate the demands but, as important as these gains are, a definition of politics that is tied too tightly to examples of protest and resistance reduces politics to an essentially negative endeavor. This understanding, on its own, would obscure the depth of the challenge we face when the enabling condition of state sovereignty itself denies the political appearance of individuals as particular speaking subjects. Politics must be conceptualized positively, so that freedom, as Arendt asserts, means "the right 'to be a participator in government,' or it means nothing." This is not easy.

PART 3 ACTION: THE PRESENCE OF POLITICS AND THE ABSENCE OF MIGRANT-HOOD

CHAIM: Who's your leader?
GEDALEH: I suppose I am. I'm the one who led the band, for better or for worse, from White Russia to here; but you see, we don't have ranks, we never have had. I've almost never needed to give orders. I would suggest something, or sometimes another person would, and we would discuss it and come to an agreement; but most of the time we found we already agreed, without discussing. We lived and fought like that, for eighteen months, and we walked for two thousand kilometers. I was their leader because I invented things, because I had the ideas and thought of the solutions; but why should we have a leader now, when the war is over and we're entering a peaceful country?

—Primo Levi, *If Not Now, When?*

This book's argument is that the condition of migrant-hood appears in the absence of political action and vice versa. This dynamic has little to do with one's formal status as a citizen or migrant, but rather with peoples' ability to overcome structural atomization and constitute public spaces on their own terms in whatever form they might take. In this very act itself, the particular person appears as such in front of others who necessarily confirm that individual's personhood. Therefore, to terminate the condition of migrant-hood is simultaneously to construct public space, to actualize people in the particular, and to therefore inaugurate political action.

As a public space is required for the particular person to appear, conversely, those spaces only materialize when people organize themselves on their own negotiated terms. Yet such positive politics is not easy because the demands of daily life prioritize the generic individual over the particular individual (as they favor cognition over thinking, *zöe* over *bios*, and animal over human). Our daily tasks have us serving economic and administrative processes that we ourselves are not empowered to define. Part 1 examined migrant-hood's enabling conditions, while in Part 2 we examined the deceptiveness of economic and administrative activity, which gives the doer a sense of agency and particularity while precluding her constitution with others. Part 3 examines the basis of a politics that depends on the particular, not the generic, individual as much as how the particular individual's own personhood depends on the opportunity to participate in politics. Without that opportunity, the individual lacks a "space of appearance" and is condemned to a life of privation, to a private life. Spaces of appearance exist only as people come together from their own particular standpoints as equals to decide what to do and to subsequently undertake action. It follows that if people are not directly involved in the (re)creation of the world they jointly inhabit, then the resulting atomization (1) reduces democracy to technocracy and so objectifies otherwise particular people; (2) generates psychological problems like depression, loneliness, and political apathy; and (3) impairs our capacity to imagine how things might be done differently. The imagination cannot develop in isolation; it requires our direct engagement with the world to give it the content with which it can conceive new possibilities. A chimera, for example, is unimaginable unless one is aware of goats, lions, and snakes.

Harrowing as it is, the concentration camp—modernity's darkest manifestation—brings these two diametrically opposed forms of sovereignty into full relief: one premised on the human qua animalized object, and the other on the human qua particular speaking subject. It therefore provides us with an example, on the one hand, of the undiluted methods with which people are robbed of personhood, condemned to migrant-hood, and made to be busy for the sake of busyness itself; and on the other, of how the seeds of direct democracy can nevertheless be sewn immediately upon the camp's collapse. The first point has been well covered in arguments explaining how modernity itself preconditions the camp, rendering it a grim expression of modernity rather than a deviation from it. I will briefly review that argument here. The second point has received noticeably less consideration. I suggest that the reason involves a cultivated ignorance of what it actually presents to us: a democracy based on ethical negotiations between people, who actualize their particularity in the very act of constitution itself, rather than a technocracy based on the expert management (and also the self-management) of animalized and equalized bodies and minds.

Regarding the first point, many theorists, Arendt, Agamben, and Bauman among them, have insisted that the essential elements of modern society crystallize into the relentless form of the concentration camp. These elements are necessary, but not sufficient reasons for the camp. They had to have been assembled in a historically particular moment that appeared in the years leading up to and including the Second World War. Some of those elements include hyperatomization, the complete erasure of the particular speaking subject, the production of rootlessness, the reduction of all action to meaningless, utilitarian activity, and the replacement of political deliberations with administrative efficiency. The inmate's experience is the ultimate form of migrant-hood.

Arendt sees the camp as the particular embodiment of totalitarianism, under which she included both fascism and Stalinism.

The victims' preparation for the camp converts them into migrants by requiring "a period of political disintegration [which] suddenly and unexpectedly made hundreds of thousands of human beings homeless, stateless, outlawed and unwanted, while millions of human beings were made economically superfluous and socially burdensome by unemployment." This transformation occurs in two steps. First, the juridical person must be eliminated thereby removing legal protection and allowing the state to treat that person as an extralegal entity. To this end, Jews were first stripped of citizenship in countries under Nazi occupation so that they could be deported without recourse to the law. The second step is to destroy the moral person. This move not only rids the person of the will to act politically, but also renders it nonsensical for anyone else to elevate the victim into a martyr around whom resistance can organize. The destruction of the moral person is complete when no compelling answer can respond to the question, "How many people here still believe that a protest has even historic importance?" Following these two steps are the monstrous methods with which the victims are treated: transported in packed cattle cars, shorn, shaved, starved, and put into drab clothing. The intentional prolongation of the moment of death completes the message that one's particular life is worthless; the individual is reduced to a living corpse among masses of living corpses.

Bauman makes clear in *Modernity and the Holocaust* that the Holocaust was unthinkable without rational and economic planning, but also that the camp functioned under a strange economic inefficiency. While, on the one hand, its activities and decisions about how long to keep its inmates alive were calculated to optimize labor power, on the other, the operation was costly to administer and its productive capacity was low. Much of what its inmates were made to do had little if any economic value. The camp itself was a testimony to bad economic planning. The point of pointless activity, as Arendt suggests, is to prove that in totalitarianism everything is possible, even that which no one thought was probable.

Hence, Agamben reasons that "Auschwitz is the existence of the impossible, the most radical negation of contingency. . . . The *Muselmann* [the "living dead" of the camp] produced by Auschwitz is the catastrophe of the subject that then follows." This catastrophe is only possible with the complete triumph of cognition over thinking. The former cannot tolerate contingency in its efforts to understand, so the demands of logical necessity, expressed as modern ideology, get violently transposed into the living world, which can be nothing other than a historically contingent world. If such total domination is achieved, then the plurality of people in the world is reduced to a common mass of identical and interchangeable individuals who operate, in Arendt's phrasing, as mere "bundles of reactions." Life is merely provoked and directed by animal-like stimulus-and-response. Only one's cognitive faculty is of interest in the camp: the technician asks, "How can I make a person do literally anything?" and the inmate asks, "How can I optimize scarce resources to survive?"

The point of reviewing the hyperrational and antipolitical foundations of the modern concentration camp is not to feel relief that they are nearly absent in the post–Cold War world. Rather, it is to clearly identify the modus operandi through which modernity as we know it steals our political capacity while keeping us busy with activity. While there may be legal and ethical restraints now in place that block a wholesale slip back to the horrors of the concentration camp (North Korea appears to be an exception), the elements that were necessary for its manifestation are still firmly with us in a neoliberal world, if only arranged in a safer configuration: busyness for busyness's sake; the privileging of cognition over thinking; the emphasis on the animalized, generic individual; the drive to do anything that technology allows, simply because it can be done; and the economic rationalization of all activity, to say nothing of the continued use of abstract categories to collectivize millions of otherwise distinct persons. Hence, the sardonic slogan that hung above the entrance to Auschwitz and other camps—*Arbeit macht frei*—mocks not only the arriving inmate, as Žižek wryly observes, but also the naïve belief in both socialist and liberal economics that work (or labor) itself is the means by which we seize control over our destinies. The slogan seems to call this belief's bluff through a gruesome use of irony: that while labor frees the body for another day of living in a rationalized world, it fundamentally kills a person's ability to constitute a world with others on their own negotiated terms. The animal lives, but the person dies.

Yet in a strange temporal proximity to the concentration camp, we find a subtle example of a founding act of political constitution that depended on the full appearance of the particular speaking subjects who undertook it. This example was not located in the camp's shadowy black market, where inmates, guards, and outsiders traded in precious commodities against its bureaucratic regulations. Rather, it appeared in the open light at precisely the moment when the camp's bureaucracy collapsed and had not yet been replaced by a more tolerant state regime. We might expect this "in-between" moment to usher in a violent "state of nature" uncontained by transcendent state structures. However, if there is wisdom to be gained in Primo Levi's account, then we find this spontaneous and foundational act in the absence of those structures altogether.

"THE FIRST DAY OF CREATION"

Levi's narration of his last ten days at Auschwitz—between the evacuation of the German forces on January 18, 1945, and the arrival of the Soviet forces on January 27—provides an invaluable case in point. This part of the story begins as the SS evacuate all inmates from Auschwitz ahead of the Soviet advance, except those who were consigned to the camp's infirmary. The *Krankenbau*, or Ka-Be as it was locally called, held eight hundred inmates (*Häftlinge*) placed into rooms according to their illness. Levi was sent to the Ka-Be for having contracted diphtheria or typhoid and shared a room there with ten others. Lacking the SS-imposed order of camp life, the remaining infirmed inmates, crippled with disease, hunger, filth, and fatigue, now had to survive in a new order that they themselves had to create. Levi described those ten days as "outside both world and time," in contrast to the previous twelve months since his arrival at Auschwitz and his later return to "normal" life.

Of the eleven inmates in Levi's room, only he and two Frenchmen, Arthur and Charles, had the strength to venture outside their barrack. Soviet bombardments began on the first night. Some of the evacuated huts caught fire, forcing inmates in adjacent barracks to flee into the cold. Many of them appeared at Levi's hut, threatening and begging to be let in. The inmates inside decided against it to prevent further degradation of the meager material conditions in which they themselves were surviving. The next morning, Levi, Charles, and Arthur left the room in search of scraps of food and other useful materials that might be lying about the camp. Just one day after the evacuation, Auschwitz had begun to decompose: no water, no electricity, broken-down buildings, iron sheets dangling from rooftops, and ashes from the fires drifting in the air. Bombs and the scavenging inmates had left the place in tatters. Rooms forbidden to the inmates on January 17 had been ransacked by the morning of the nineteenth. From the kitchen, they were able to secure only two sacks of potatoes, but they found a heavy cast-iron stove in usable condition. Levi transported it back to their room in a wheelbarrow, which proved an enormous undertaking given its weight and his frail condition. With wood, coal, and embers from the burnt huts, they were able to light the stove and boil the potatoes in water melted from snow. Levi observed that "something seemed to relax in everyone."

One of the roommates, named Towarowski (a twenty-three-year-old Franco-Pole), suggested that each of the roommates offer Levi, Charles, and Arthur a slice of bread for the work they had done. Levi notes that such a gesture would have been "inconceivable" on the previous day and that this change of ethics signified the death of the concentration camp at Auschwitz. The law of the camp had been, "Eat your bread, and if you can, that of your neighbour." He added that this law "left no room for gratitude." (Note that Hobbes's savage state of nature appears *inside* the dark heart of the state-Leviathan, not *outside* of it, if we accept the tenet that the camp crystallizes modernity's modus operandi.) However, a stronger message than simple gratitude appears in Levi's telling of this particular event: "It really meant that the Lager [camp] was dead." This gesture, he relays, marks the beginnings of their transformation from "*Häftlinge* to men again." Yet this transformation, we should be aware, occurred outside of rationalized, bureaucratized society altogether, not simply outside of the camp.

When the temperature began to drop as nightfall approached, other inmates again crowded around the door wanting access to the warm stove. Charles, among the healthiest of those remaining in the camp, blocked their entry with his body in the door frame. Levi and his roommates did not fear contact per se with other ill individuals. Moreover, the thought that they themselves could find a room with less contagious diseases did not occur to them, as they were satisfied with what they had achieved in their own barrack. Sheer survival does not appear to have been Levi's, and presumably Arthur's and Charles's, only motivation to deny access. Levi explains, "The stove, our creation, was here, and spread a wonderful warmth; I had my bed here; and by now a tie united us, the eleven patients of the *Infektionsabteilung*." He describes how he and Arthur smoked cigarettes made of herbs from the kitchen and spoke of things both past and future. Living "outside both world and time" between the German army's evacuation and the Soviet army's arrival, Levi explains that "we felt at peace with ourselves and with the world." This peace was not one of resignation, that tranquility one feels when giving up the fight against some future inevitability. Rather, Levi describes it as something like a peace experienced as part of constituting a place where they could be with others as themselves. In Levi's words, "We were broken by tiredness, but seemed to have finally accomplished something useful—perhaps like God after the first day of creation." They had no other choice; they would likely have perished if they had reverted to the old law of the camp: Eat your bread and that of your neighbor's if you can.

We should not naïvely read Levi's story through the familiar narrative of determined individuals persevering against staggering odds. The individual loses this fight far more often than not. His own physical survival, as Levi made clear, had mostly to do with luck. The operative lesson is not that people will inevitably summon up the will to rebuild themselves after a journey through hell. Rather, it is, first, that merely surviving as *homo sacer* is unsatisfying for an individual regardless of the abundance or deprivation of his material circumstances; and second, that the difference between *Häftlinge* and a full person is not simply a capacity to share with others even when deprived, but rather that individuals come to life, a qualified political life, when they are partners in constituting the world they inhabit. The importance that Levi attributes to the world he created with his colleagues, when their biological survival was uncertain, testifies to a human impulse to do more than merely extend one's lifespan another day. Rather, it reveals the fulfillment of political being as an act of beginning anew with others. Created in the ashes of Auschwitz, their world was neither a utopic Garden of Eden nor free from outside events. They made the ethically questionable decision to deny warmth, food, and resources to others, a decision they made again after January 19 and prior to the arrival of Soviet forces. Yet in deciding, as a group of equals, how they should plot their course, they transformed themselves from migrants—or, more appropriate to their context, *Häftlinge*—into men. To be sure, their achievement was not utopian but surprisingly mundane.

This transition occurred so quickly that it could not be explained as a result of socialization into a new behavioral pattern.

Within two days, eleven men who had mastered the game of hyperindividualized survival of the fittest jettisoned those behavioral strategies in favor of a local democracy in the truest sense of the term: insisting on political equality among fundamentally different people. Participation did not require sensitivity training or formal education. It simply unfolded as a reasonable and fulfilling course of affairs between them. The instant transformation of the rules of the game from an obscene technocracy to an exemplary democracy happened at an unusual and revealing moment. It did not transpire in a sequence of events beginning with a prewar "normal" society to a totalitarian society to a concentration camp and back again to normal society. Rather, it happened at a point when the rationalized procedures that underpin each step in that sequence were missing. These individuals therefore ended their condition of migrant-hood when they could simply appear before each other as equal, but different, people, thereby establishing a public space in which they spoke and acted.

Levi's story testifies to his and his colleagues' endurance. It also exemplifies that the establishment of a public space does not require heroic figures but only an opportunity for people to satisfy an impulse to organize a place for themselves in the world. That desire cannot actualize itself in private, even under wealthy circumstances. Levi and his colleagues ceased being migrants the moment they assembled around the stove and were astute enough to ask if that experience resembled how God felt on the first day of creation. We should not read the metaphor of God's miracle of creation with either reverence or cynicism. This "miracle" symbolizes the quintessentially human capacity to inaugurate a new chain of events, just as God's creation of the earth was unprecedented. Unlike other animals, humans have the potential to (re)constitute themselves and set history off in a new direction that is not solely determined by the need to maintain the body's circular, metabolic demands. This moment did not reveal a simple animalistic will to survive. Rather, it signified a moment when a group of human beings elevated themselves above the animal realm and performed the uniquely human act of constituting a world that did not exist before.

THE JOY OF THE NEW

The path to action draws together three elements within the particular individual and with which Levi and his colleagues constituted a sovereign space of appearance. The faculty of thinking demanded that they assess their situation from the standpoints of those tied to their circumstances. The faculty of judgment demanded that they decide what to do in the absence of a tradition, a law, or a code of conduct to instruct them. Finally, their *wills* brought them forth into action. Thinking itself makes no appearance in the world as it occurs in solitude. The thinker may reach agreement with himself through the two-in-one dialogue, but this unification alone does not beget political action. He must conjure up the will to act or to speak in his own voice and have his unity, and so his integrity, recognized by others. However, like the thinking subject, the will is not unified either. The will to act is always met with an internal countervailing will not to act. As Augustine explains the dilemma, the mind can control the body, as the body moves the instant that the mind so commands. In contrast, the mind commands itself and it is met instantly with resistance. He writes in *Confessions*, "We are dealing with a morbid condition of the mind which, when lifted up by the truth, does not unreservedly rise to it but is weighed down by habit. So there are two wills. Neither of them is complete, and what is present in the one is lacking in the other." The individual only becomes complete when the decision to act is instantiated in practice after one's will to act prevails over the will to refrain. At this point, the thinking dialogue ends and the individual finally discloses his particular identity to the public before him. In their treatment of him as an equal, but particular person, he comes to life through the polity he has constituted with them. However, he would have no political life without the will to present himself in front of others who concretize that unity as a particular and singular figure in their act of recognition.

These particular people, now so constituted, move history in a rectilinear direction, where by definition it cannot have gone before. Their freedom and appearance have coalesced in that foundational act itself. This miracle of human creation is the embodiment of human *being* itself: the capacity to inaugurate the new by stepping past two forms of time that enslave human beings. On the one hand, it frees the actors from the chains of circular time that bind us qua laboring bodies to the circular demands of biological and social reproduction; that is, living for the sake of living and no more. On the other, it frees those actors from modernity's linear time in which history allegedly moves in a straight, pregiven direction under natural or historical law but for that very reason requires the presence of no particular person to move it forward. Both temporal situations are antithetical to political action and, it follows, to the appearance of any particular person in the world. For these reasons, Augustine reasons that God did not make Man *in* the course of time but rather that time began with the creation of human beings, because the essence of being human is to inaugurate time with unprecedented actions. Otherwise, we experience time as a standstill in which nothing foundational happens or, similarly, as a treadmill in which all energy is devoted to exercising the body into health but yet never gets us anywhere despite the laborious effort.

The record of such examples of joint political action is unnecessarily scarce. On the one hand, people rarely have opportunities to assemble themselves on such a basis so there is some reason not to expect an extensive record of it. On the other, the scarcity reflects a failure to recognize such foundational acts when they do appear, which is more often than we might think. This situation precludes the emergence of a cultural narrative and a political philosophy (if David Graeber and Hannah Arendt, respectively, are to be believed—the latter writing in the 1950s and 1960s) into which these acts can be bestowed to future generations. Rather than constantly reinvented like the proverbial wheel, they would instead appear as the normal course of events.

Graeber notes that we have little experience in creating a culture of democracy, and in the hope of rectifying that problem, he points to numerous examples, in the form of anarchist movements and direct democracies, that go unnoticed, misrepresented, and wrongly maligned. (The democracies on pirate ships sailing on the margins of colonial trade routes makes a particularly strong impression.) These appear regularly throughout history, but often in the margins of rationalized societies. They represent examples of Hardt and Negri's "multitude" in action because in the fleeting moments of their association they are not in contract with a transcendent sovereign being and so they become politically self-determined. No doubt a popular misunderstanding of the term "anarchism" itself contributes to the dearth of awareness about what it has to offer. Graeber defines anarchy with nonthreatening simplicity: any "form of organization that does not involve ultimate recourse to bureaucratic structures of violence" and, as he consistently highlights, maintains a horizontal form of social organization. He points out that anarchy itself has left little theoretical tradition to invoke, in contrast to Marxism, because it does not trace its lineage back to a single thinker presenting the world with a utopic future. Rather, anarchy is best characterized by its own egalitarian practices leaving people themselves to work out the type of association they desire. For this reason, Graeber explains that anarchism, in contrast to the other big ideas of the nineteenth century, made the most sense to people in the world beyond Europe. We should claim as anarchy's legacy its methods of deliberation and take counsel that it is neither so naïve as to offer a utopia nor so cynical as to settle for a dystopia of nihilist individuals who only gratify their own interests.

However, to say that anarchism lacks a utopic theoretical tradition does not mean that it would not benefit from theoretical insights linking personhood to political action. Arendt, whose writings after *Eichmann in Jerusalem* focus on the question of political being unconstrained by bureaucratic conditions, routinely lauded the diverse and spontaneous associations that people themselves undertook in moments of rupture. She likewise decried the way professional revolutionaries robbed them of their political potency by absorbing their efforts into party apparatuses, which were modeled on the same bureaucratic states they meant to overthrow. She applauded Jefferson's ward system and similar versions of it that appeared in different circumstances elsewhere in time and place. These included the revolutionary societies and municipal councils that spread across France early into the 1789 revolution; the councils that arose during the 1871 Paris Commune, and in 1905 during the first Russian Revolution and again in 1917; the *Rätesystem* and *Räterepublick* that formed in Germany after the First World War; and the council systems that emerged during the 1956 Hungarian Revolution. In each of these examples—featuring peasants, workers, students, coffeehouse intellectuals, soldiers, and civil servants—people turned their own accidental proximity to each other into a political organization particular to the situation in which they were immersed. Like contemporary anarchists, these people in all their heterogeneity do not represent simply "the poor," but rather anyone whom institutionalized power renders voiceless. In this regard, they resemble the "multitude" insofar as they are trapped within the mechanisms of social production, leaving them to function *as* mechanisms and no more. The frustration that spills onto the streets in the myriad of unrelated examples, then, is not simply the desire for scarce resources. Rather, it is the demand that the particular people undertaking action become constituent parts of government, however it may be arranged. To be such a constituent subject is to be fully present as a free and thinking subject.

Many critical intellectuals have expressed their skepticism toward the various councils that Arendt held up as positive examples of politics through spontaneous association, all the while commending her critique of how modernity has systematically obstructed their possibility. (Anarchism confronts a similar critique.) For them, either it is a romantic read of history or it fails to account for the larger structural relations of inequality that shot through local councils. However, Jacques Rancière's pragmatic view of democratic politics as rooted in actual practices of equality pushes back. From his *Disagreement: Politics and Philosophy*, he argues that "politics, in the fully specific sense of the term, is rare. It is always local and provisional." In an interview with Eric Hazan he continues to say, "I am trying to convey that democracy, in the sense of the power of the people, the power of those who have no special entitlement to exercise power, is the very basis of what makes politics thinkable. . . . Equality exists through that, in actuality, and not as [a] goal we might reach if we had the right strategy or the right leadership or the right science. Frankly, I don't see why that stance is bleaker than any other." If we conclude that people cannot self-organize locally and democratically, then we can only lapse back into technocracies that have driven modern history to its current place. These all operate on the condescending premise that particular people cannot govern themselves. Naïveté is not a compelling counterpoint unless the actors have not soberly assessed the situation they confront. In any case, all action requires some amount of naïveté because action, by definition, means heading into unchartered territory for which there is no reliable rule book. Failure is a likely prospect, but even failed attempts bequeath the gift of experience.

Critically, institutions and political action are not necessarily in contradiction. If they were, then political action could never create a stable place for people to be in the world. If institutions are defined by those who compose them, then they provide a reliable forum in which those same people can congregate. If the ethical lines that previously underscored their association do not apply to new situations, then the institution does not preclude their redrawing those lines because they themselves are poised to reconstitute that institution and so move in a new direction. Here the multitude, or the plurality of speaking subjects organized around common concerns, safeguards the passage from revolt to revolutionary institution, as Hardt and Negri aptly phrase the problem. While the term "revolutionary" evokes a wide variety of emotional and conflicting responses, it fundamentally refers to the human capacity to begin something new, which arguably is the defining characteristic of *being* human. Institutions are only alienating if the people whom they serve do not themselves constitute them, and so cannot reconstitute them differently whenever necessary. Crucial to this arrangement is that the state in which the actors are organized must follow their actions, and not the other way around, lest the actors have their activities determined by the state.

However, such modes of political action easily dissipate back into rationalized modes of policymaking and party politics; further, they usually lack a record of what they achieved and how they did it. These losses can be largely attributed to the fact that the concept of state sovereignty still orients our understanding of politics and resistance. We are not poised to recognize and appreciate what other political forms have to offer. (It should be emphasized that "other" forms were the focus of classic political anthropology. While that approach is subject to valid postcolonial critiques, it nevertheless recognized alternative political subjectivities, that is, different ways of being a political actor.) In this vein, anthropologist Michael Herzfeld lucidly demonstrates in *Cultural Intimacy* the intertwining of state ideology and everyday life which efficiently "converts revolution into conformity, represents ethnic cleansing as national consensus and cultural homogeneity, and recasts the sordid terrors of emergence into a seductive immortality." Here power and resistance are contained within the same frame.

Further explaining this lack of political imagination, Arendt observes that the Western tradition of political philosophy itself has held political action in contempt as something involving only petty interests and disregard for final truths on which a reliably stable society can be built. She notes with her usual candor that "what is remarkable among all great thinkers is the difference in rank between their political philosophies and the rest of their works—even in Plato. Their politics never reaches the same depth. This lack of depth is nothing but a failure to sense the depths in which politics is anchored." For example, although Plato's *Republic* can be read in multiple ways, the dominant interpretation holds that the thinker leaves the darkness of the cave, in which human experience is but flickering shadows on a wall, to revel in divinely abstract forms. He only reluctantly returns as the philosopher-king to nobly rule the polis, composed of people who cannot govern themselves. This utopic vision has no need for action because the philosopher-king is endowed with the eternal knowledge necessary to justly advise and manage. Jean-Luc Nancy reinforces Arendt's point with his equally shrewd perception that "over the whole span from the Greeks to us, politics has implied the mere regulation of common existence, on one hand, and some sort of heavenly assumption into the meaning or truth of this existence, on the other. One moment politics is clearly demarcating its own sphere of action where it claims authority, the next it is pushing to take charge of the totality of existence, individual and collective."

To illustrate the lost legacies (and so the lost possibilities) of positive political action, Arendt recalls the words of René Char, French poet and member of the *Résistance*: "If I survive, I know that I shall have to break with the aroma of these essential years, silently reject (not repress) my treasure." This treasure was the public space that these men and women had to create for themselves as they lived in hidden spaces during the war. They were outside of occupied France and living more freely than they had prior to the war. Yet liberation from Nazi forces only returned Char and his colleagues to a sadly opaque, private life consumed with nothing but itself. Former comrades separated into the ideological cliques of postwar party politics. They no longer constituted a public in which each need not suspect his own self of "insincerity" and of being "a carping, suspicious actor of life." These exiles qua exiles found the "apparition of freedom" as Arendt describes it. This discovery was not the result of fighting against the occupation as every Allied soldier undertook that endeavor. Rather, as exiles they had taken the initiative to create a public space in which freedom could appear: "At every meal that we eat together, freedom is invited to sit down. The chair remains vacant, but the place is set."

It is important to recognize, pace Benhabib, that the example of René Char and the lost revolutionary tradition is not a romantic yearning for spontaneous association. Rather, it reveals a confidence that nothing prevents people from constituting public space if they are not precluded by mass society's condition of migranthood. As shown even in Primo Levi's example, perfect worlds will never be created, but the impossibility of creating a utopia does not rob us of political agency. What robs us is an inability to modify, when needed, the basic ethical tenets of our world because structural atomization has precluded joint action. The challenge, similarly, is not to find the right ideology or even an institutional blueprint, but rather to create the conditions in which people negotiate how to institutionalize themselves. When they are so empowered, they create a stable ethics to premise their future actions, which they can also change as necessary when new situations require unprecedented responses.

How do we know we are engaged in political action when it happens? What is the affective experience of *being* fully present in an act of (re)constitution with others? The answer might seem somewhat underwhelming. However, this only testifies to how mundane our experience with political action could be (but is not), and also how strange the experience of migrant-hood should be (but also is not). Perhaps the answer, similarly strange but mundane, is the particular kind of thrill, enjoyment, and sense of possibility in its undertaking. Graeber points out that in anarchist movements "it is difficult to find anyone who has fully participated in such an action whose sense of human possibilities has not been profoundly transformed as a result. It's one thing to say, 'Another world is possible.' It's another to experience it, however momentarily." He puts forth the reasonable conviction, as mundane as it is profound, "that free people really ought to be able to sit down together like reasonable adults and govern their own affairs." It resembles the sense of creation and even deep relaxation that Levi and his colleagues sensed as they warmed themselves around the stove. Arendt similarly recounts how American revolutionaries wrote about the happiness of founding a new republic in their letters to each other. In Jefferson's playful correspondence with Adams about what an afterlife might entail, he concludes, "May we meet there again, in Congress, with our antient Colleagues, and receive with them the seal of approbation 'Well done, good and faithful servants.'" She parallels Jefferson's reply to Socrates, who in the *Apology* similarly wishes for an afterlife much like the life he had lived. He sought no blessed island where he could rest his soul, but rather the enlargement of the circle of interlocutors with whom he could engage in unending dialogues about the best way for people to live together. The experience itself—of struggling to constitute worlds with others—cannot be rivaled by anything beyond an earthly life, not even the liberation from fear, pain, and worry that an afterlife might bring. Critics will rightly argue that slavery and oppression upheld the polities in which people like Jefferson and Socrates could enjoy fulfilling experiences with political action. However, the lasting lesson should be the path they chose given the political conditions in which they acted. They could have pursued many different forms of politics, including tyranny or kingship, that would have bequeathed no notion at all that politics can be a transformative and worthy pursuit; these other directions would have gone no further in eradicating slavery even still. Instead, their paths depended on an understanding that a particular mode of being in the world is required to make political action attractive to individuals qua particular speaking subjects. That political modality can speak to injustices better than any other, even if slavery is one that it sadly missed in these examples.

The joy of political action should not be taken for granted. It may go much more easily than it may come, but in any case it depends on the human capacity to inaugurate new chains of events. Returning to *Waiting for the Barbarians*, we find Coetzee ending the novel with a curious but tenuous serenity. The Empire's troops and sadistic administrators flee the outpost as winter arrives and their campaign disintegrates. With his torture now behind him, the magistrate ultimately finds himself trying to record a history of what his town will leave for posterity. After a few unsatisfying starts, he thinks to himself, "There has been something staring me in the face, and I still do not see it." He walks across the barracks yard in the snowfall to where the town's children are building a snowman in the middle of the square, precisely where the "barbarians" were tortured. He is anxious not to alarm them, but feels, in his words, "inexplicably joyful" as he approaches them, while they assemble the head with its eyes, ears, nose, and mouth and crown it with a cap. The snowman metaphorically represents not just *bare life* (again, *zöe*, the human-animal, life itself, and so on), but rather *a particular life* with a particular face unlike the face of anyone else. Indeed, the magistrate hardly interacts with the children throughout the book but rather stares at them from time to time. Like the adult inhabitants of the town, they rarely make an assertive appearance. However, unlike the adults, they are often jointly engaged in creative activity such as the building of snow forts, the metaphorical constitution of a polity. They do this playful work without prompting from adults, but rather as a joint spontaneous action, even if it is politically neutral since they are only children.

Coetzee is too shrewd an observer to naïvely place hope in children simply because they are children. While the children are clearly the most creative individuals in the story, they are also easily corruptible. They are encouraged to participate in the beating of the barbarians in the town square, and they eagerly watch the spectacle of the magistrate himself being hanged because it is obviously important, though they do not understand the reason. He nevertheless ends the novel with children engaged in a playful act of constitution so as to keep alive the possibility of a new beginning incumbent in each new particular life that appears on earth. Children can go either way, which means they can go the route of direct political action as they do during play. Like the anarchists that Graeber describes, like Char, like Jefferson, and like Socrates, children also find a thrill in directly constituting a place for themselves in the world if only in play. That thrill sadly dissipates once the game is over, as witnessed when they must go home for dinner after having built towns together out of cardboard boxes, or out of branches in the woods, or out of sand dunes at a beach. The thrill exists only in the action itself because each individual's own particularity takes on a concrete reality in the eyes of the others with whom they play as equal but different children.

THE SPACE OF APPEARANCE AND THE ABSENCE OF MIGRANT·HOOD

In this context, it becomes easier to appreciate that political action is what emancipates the individual from loneliness and atomization. This emancipation occurs not when a lost soul joins a mass movement, but rather when joint political action transpires through the direct deliberations of speaking subjects. In the deliberative act itself, each particular individual gains recognition from the others thus creating a space for these actors in a durable world of their own making that will coalesce around the historical narratives they will tell to record their actions. They are migrants no longer. The intersubjective character of positive politics—that particular individuals obtain a worldly reality only through mutual recognition of each other as speaking and acting subjects—has a remarkably mundane basis. Jean-Luc Nancy could add, "All that we can know boils down to two propositions: our existence is without any prior design, destiny, or project; and it is neither individual nor collective, since existence, the truth of 'being' is something that only comes about within the plurality of individuals into which dissolves any postulate of the unity of 'being.'"

If joint political action undermines the condition of migrant-hood, then the tactical question of how such a capacity for action may be institutionalized takes on paramount importance. Again, action and institution mutually support each other when the individuals composing the institution are empowered to decide its purpose and meaning. This premise stands in contrast to transcendental sovereign forms in which the give-and-take of positive politics gets reduced to administrative reason and the application of pregiven formulas. We should not be surprised if no singular institutional model comes forth, but rather a variety of situationally specific institutions that people create to ensure the political equality of all participants. In their variety of forms these institutions would signify, to various extents, "spaces of appearance." Graeber's description of how people in anarchist movements reach political decisions illustrates how participants constitute such a place in the world. His descriptions would seem applicable to what Hardt and Negri call "militancy": a constituent activity, not a representational one, that is positive, constructive, and innovative and actualized against imperial command. Decision is done by consensus rather than by majority vote, through such organizational forms as spokes-councils, break-outs, fishbowls, blocking concerns, and vibewatchers. As the group deliberates, views that fall outside an emerging consensus are pared away until a course of action is agreed on. Because consensus is not perfectly obtainable, proposals that are not accepted by all should at least not strike anyone as highly objectionable. Graeber highlights that decisions proceed in an egalitarian manner, one in which particular views enjoy a safeguarded space of appearance. This method only works if everyone speaks and all voices are fairly considered in the deliberations. Finding consensus involves acts of persuasion and a willingness to be persuaded so that people can adjust their positions to reach an agreement that might have been unforeseeable. People actualize themselves as particular speaking subjects in these deliberations, though not merely because they assert their opinions. Instead, the deliberations concretize the existence of each particular individual through the act of engaging each other as speakers and listeners. Contrary to its reputation of destruction and negativity, the lesson of anarchism is that political action is a positive endeavor, something more than resistance against the institutionalized practices it challenges, insofar as it creates a situation in which people themselves are empowered to constitute (and reconstitute as necessary) their polity. Political action thus eliminates the condition of migrant-hood and the structural conditions of loneliness by enabling the unique individual to appear in the world through joint action.

Despite the important postmodern critiques, the classic literature in political anthropology also shows similar egalitarianism within traditional hunter-gatherer bands. Like those that migrated out of Africa, these groups have something to teach us about spaces of appearance. While Graeber is correct that "we" must learn a culture of democracy, that literature also indicates that such cultures appear as a matter of course, even if only to varying degrees and in differing permutations, outside the reach of modernity's atomizing effects. Similar to anarchist movements within the modernist frame, these bands operated without formal leadership and instead took the advice of those having strong aptitudes for the tasks at hand. Political decisions were arrived at through direct deliberations. Deference may have been given to elders (or to anyone with an aptitude for something pertinent to the discussion), but elders could not maintain legitimacy by insisting on their own viewpoint in the face of someone else's sound argument.

In the 1950s, Peristiany illustrated a similar point when describing the decision-making procedures of the Kipsigi, a cattle-herding society in highland Kenya. Kipsigi society is largely built on three institutions: a patrilineage, a military regiment (largely defunct at the time of his writing), and an age-set of coevals that cut across territorial village units. Peristiany asks how the Kipsigi deal with problems that affect society as a whole and not just sectional groups. Such problems are resolved by a council of elders. Members do not derive their office through appointment or from a higher authority; rather, the council is composed of men who owe their prestige to age, wisdom, character, and patronage through marriage and cattle exchange. They court public opinion by appealing to the values which traditionally hold the broader society together. While this may sound typical of any politician in the mass nation-state, the techniques by which they do so involve knowledge of particular persons rather than stereotyped acts of false solidarity such as hugging babies or eating donuts in diners. The elders know well both the litigants and the means by which their cattle—the basis of the Kipsigi economy—have been acquired. Peristiany tells the story of one elder who could trace the progeny of a litigant's cow over three generations.

A decision must satisfy the council, the plaintiff, and the defendant, and it will necessarily amount to a compromise between ideal conceptions of Kipsigi moral order and the current social reality. Tailoring judgments to the particular conditions in which a crime occurred, then, is essential to a wise council. Social ideals can be reinterpreted as necessary rather than slavishly followed regardless of circumstances. Peristiany notes that Kipsigis must see European courts of law as rigid, abstract, and inhumane for their insistence on the integrity of first principles and their commitment to retribution. In that system, judgment takes on a deductive character and lessens the need for a council in the first place. In other words, it favors the faculty of cognition over the faculty of thinking, thereby mooting the ethical judgments and need for persuasion. The Kipsigi council, were it to follow the European courts, would be reduced to administrators rather than people reexamining moral order from particular standpoints. In the Kipsigi situation, litigants cannot defy the council's judgment because it is deeply rooted in the wider social field. In contrast to state-based jurisprudence, the Kipsigi individual cannot be easily isolated and punished. His very connections to others constitute the fabric of society itself, unlike a society constituted by an economic/administrative apparatus into which atomized individuals must fit themselves. Challenging the Kipsigi council's judgment would risk schism in society or ostracization from it. Peristiany describes these possibilities as "grave sanctions." If someone continues to be a troublemaker, he will meet the consternation of his neighbors, who may boycott his family. This may result in his own lineage expelling him. A matter most grave, Peristiany explains, such a man becomes the equivalent of a man without citizenship, rendering him the equivalent of Agamben's *homo sacer*.

A strong similarity appears between Kipsigi deliberation and anarchist deliberations. Graeber explains that anarchism amounts to a movement between three poles: an attitude toward existing circumstances; a vision of how the world should be to rectify those circumstances; and a set of practices that ensure egalitarian procedures for moving in that direction. However, since the vision of the world does not dominate this tripartite arrangement, it can be changed by reconciling different perspectives so that a new vision emerges out of egalitarian procedures. Similarly, since the technical, deliberative practices do not dominate the arrangement, daily life is not reduced to mere administrative and economic activity governed by a singular, instrumental logic; instead, continuous efforts are made to approximate daily life to an agreed-on vision in order to rectify the problem. This movement between poles transpires directly between people, since people qua particular beings work off each other rather than deduce their ethics and "action plans" from unquestionable norms and forms. Philosophically, the process illustrates the importance of Kant's *exemplary validity*, in which general principles are found in the common features of actually existing phenomena. If we decide that a table qua table is an object with a flat surface elevated on four legs, then we have abstracted a principle from empirical observations. However, since we ourselves decided on that principle as inferred from our different standpoints, then we are also empowered to redefine table qua table if we decide it necessary due to new situations and changes in perspectives.

Arendt's spaces of appearance, thinking through exemplary validity, find expression in different variants of anarchist movements, in the Kipsigi, and in countless other societies that are not organized on the basis of an allegedly homogenous population. People qua individuals constitute spaces of appearance by negotiating the terms of their coexistence. The polity requires *thinking*, or again, the search for meaning in ambiguous circumstances by inspecting other people's viewpoints. A space of appearance results from people's direct deliberations, in the form of willful action and speech, for the sake of (re)creating the basis of their coexistence in the "polity." A term long abandoned in favor of "society," "polity" need not refer to a bounded "polis" composed of citizens per se. Rather, "it is the organization of the people as it arises out of acting and speaking together . . . no matter where they happen to be." It is a space of appearance in which particular individuals are recognized as such by others with whom they speak and act while they (re)constitute the basis of their common assembly. Crucially, this recognition implies an openness to being transformed by others lest one's own immutability reinforce one's isolation even in the physical proximity of others. Thus, a failure to recognize others in the polity—or indeed refraining from trying to constitute a polity with others—also diminishes oneself by evaporating the space of appearance.

Action requires that we ethically judge particular situations according to the context in which they appear, namely, as unprecedented events that cannot be comprehended through pregiven moral tenets (that is, deductively and cognitively). To judge requires the solicitation of alternative viewpoints about which one must think, though not with automatic empathy or without critical examination. It requires us to amass these alternatives in order to gain as wide an array of perspectives as possible. The public validity of the subsequent judgment is "neither universal nor subjective, depending on personal whim, but intersubjective and representative." The appeal to the community, or polity, to which one belongs is based on deliberation with others (not on universal moral codes, abstract policy templates, or market value). It necessarily allows the speaker to appear as a particular individual poised to persuade (and be persuaded by) others as to how they can best organize their coexistence in the polity. The resulting action constitutes what Arendt calls the *vita activa* by virtue of its very performance. By definition, it is "new" because it is decided on the basis of a particular judgment about a particular situation determined in dialogue with a plurality of persons and perspectives. The polity's intersubjective quality satisfies an impulse to appear in public and to escape atomization. It transforms people from generic, speechless objects to particular speaking subjects and inherently creates public space in the very act of deliberation. One cannot evade the condition of migrant-hood unless one constitutes such a space of appearance with others. The achievement here would be to overturn a fundamental tension in the modern trajectory itself, which Hardt and Negri describe as the tension between the immanent plane of lived, earthly reality in all of its plurality and the notion of transcendent, sovereign authority, emerging first in Europe's absolute monarchies and later in the nation-state. This tension forms Jean Bodin's paradox that if people in the plural were to rule, then there would be no sovereignty, because no singular figure could transcend the others, thus undermining what became modern state sovereignty. Its resolution is found in the space of appearance in which sovereignty is not obtained by appeal to transcendent authority, but rather in the negotiated agreements and willful actions based on people's own faculty of judgment and powers of persuasion. It is here where the existential question, *Do I really matter in this world?* is finally answered in the affirmative. This existential question, too easily dismissed as a personal question only, is instead the very basis of freedom and the beginning of the end of migrant-hood.

BIBLIOGRAPHY

Agamben, Giorgio. *Homo Sacer: Sovereign Power and Bare Life*. Trans. Daniel Heller-Roazen. Stanford, CA: Stanford University Press, 1998.

———. *Remnants of Auschwitz*. New York: Zone Books, 1999.

Anderson, Benedict. *Imagined Communities: Reflections on the Origins and Spread of Nationalism*. London: Verso, 1983.

Arendt, Hannah. "The Conquest of Space and the Stature of Man," in *Between Past and Future*, pp. 260–274. New York: Penguin Books, 2006.

———. *The Human Condition*. Chicago: University of Chicago Press, 1998.

———. *Lectures on Kant's Political Philosophy*. Ed. Ronald Beiner. Chicago: University of Chicago Press, 1982.

———. *The Life of the Mind*. San Diego: Harcourt Brace Jovanovich, 1978.

———. *On Revolution*. New York: Penguin Books, 2006.

———. *The Origins of Totalitarianism*. San Diego: Harcourt Brace Jovanovich, 1968.

———. *The Promise of Politics*. Ed. Jerome Kohn. New York: Schocken Books, 2005.

————. *Responsibility and Judgment.* Edited and with an intro-
duction by Jerome Kohn. New York: Schocken Books, 2003.

————. "Thinking and Moral Considerations: A Lecture." *Social
Research* 38, no. 3 (1971): 417–446.

Aristotle. *Nicomachean Ethics.* Trans. Terence Irwin. Indianapolis,
IN: Hackett, 1985.

————. *Politics.* Grinnell, IA: Peripatetic Press, 1986.

Augustine. *City of God.* London: Penguin Books, 2003.

————. *Confessions.* Oxford, UK, and New York: Oxford University Press, 1992.

————. *On Free Choice of the Will.* Indianapolis, IN: Bobbs-
Merrill, 1964.

Bauman, Zygmunt. *Modernity and the Holocaust.* Ithaca, NY:
Cornell University Press, 2001.

Beckett, Samuel. *Waiting for Godot.* New York: Grove Press, 1982.

Benhabib, Seyla. *The Reluctant Modernism of Hannah Arendt.* Lan-
ham, MD: Rowman & Littlefield, 2000.

Billig, Michael. *Banal Nationalism.* London: Sage, 1995.

Boorstin, Daniel. *The Americans: The National Experience.* New
York: Vintage Books, 1965.

British Broadcasting Company. "In Our Time: Politeness." BBC
Radio 4. September 30, 2004. http://www.bbc.co.uk/programmes/
p004y29m

Calhoun, Craig, and John McGowan. "Hannah Arendt and the
Meaning of Politics." In *Hannah Arendt and the Meaning of
Politics.* Ed. Craig Calhoun and John McGowan, pp. 1–24.
Minneapolis: University of Minnesota Press, 1997.

Camus, Albert. *The Myth of Sisyphus: And Other Essays.* New York:
Vintage Books, 1991.

Coetzee, John Maxwell. *Waiting for the Barbarians.* London: Vintage Books, 2004.

Comaroff, Jean, and John Comaroff, eds. *Law and Disorder in the
Postcolony.* Chicago: University of Chicago Press, 2006.

Feldman, Gregory. "The Specific Intellectual's Pivotal Position: Action, Compassion, and Thinking in Administrative Society, an Arendtian View." *Social Anthropology* 21, no. 2 (2013): 135–164.

Foucault, Michel. *The Birth of Biopolitics: Lectures at the Collège de France, 1978–79.* Ed. Michel Senellart et al.; trans. Graham Burchell. New York: Palgrave Macmillan, 2008.

———. *Power/Knowledge: Selected Interviews and Other Writings 1972–1977.* Ed. Colin Gordon. New York: Pantheon Books, 1980.

———. *Security, Territory, Population: Lectures at the Collège de France, 1977–78.* Ed. Michael Senellart; trans. Graham Burchell. New York: Palgrave Macmillan, 2007.

"Going off the Rails." *The Economist,* November 30, 2013, p. 67.

Graeber, David. *The Democracy Project: A History, a Crisis, a Movement.* New York: Spiegel & Grau, 2013.

———. *Direct Action: An Ethnography.* Oakland, CA: AK Press, 2009.

———. "The New Anarchists." *New Left Review* 13 (2002): 61–73. http://newleftreview.org/II/13/david-graeber-the-new-anarchists

———. "Turning Modes of Production Inside Out: Or, Why Capitalism Is a Transformation of Slavery." *Critique of Anthropology* 26, no. 1 (2006): 61–85.

Hardt, Michael, and Antonio Negri. *Commonwealth.* Cambridge, MA: Belknap Press, Harvard University Press, 2008.

———. *Empire.* Cambridge, MA: Harvard University Press, 2000.

———. *Multitude.* New York: Penguin Books, 2004.

Herzfeld, Michael. *Cultural Intimacy: Social Poetics in the Nation-State,* 2nd ed. New York: Routledge, 2005.

———. *The Social Production of Indifference: Exploring the Symbolic Roots of Western Bureaucracy.* Chicago: University of Chicago Press, 1993.

Homer. *The Iliad.* Trans. Robert Fitzgerald. New York: Anchor Books, 1974.

————. *The Odyssey*. Trans. Robert Fitzgerald. New York: Vintage Books, 1990.

Hustwit, Gary (dir.). "Objectified." Plexi Productions, 2009.

Jackson, Michael. *Existential Anthropology: Events, Exigencies and Effects*. New York and Oxford, UK: Berghahn Books, 2005.

Kristeva, Julia. *Hannah Arendt: Life Is a Narrative*. Toronto: University of Toronto Press, 2001.

Lampedusa, Giuseppe di. *The Leopard*. Trans. Archibald Colquhoun. Foreword and appendix translated by Guido Waldman, 2007. New York: Pantheon, 1960.

Levi, Primo. *If Not Now When?* Trans. William Weaver. New York: Penguin, 1995.

————. *Survival in Auschwitz*. Trans. Stuart Woolf. New York: Simon & Schuster, 1996. Originally published as *Se questo è un uomo* (1958).

Malkki, Liisa. "Refugees and Exile: From 'Refugee Studies' to the National Order of Things." *Annual Review of Anthropology* 24 (1995): 495–523.

Marx, Karl. *Capital: Volume 1*. Trans. Ben Fowkes. New York: Vintage Books, 1977.

————. *Early Writings*. Trans. and ed. T. B. Bottomore. New York: McGraw-Hill, 1964.

Nancy, Jean-Luc. "Finite and Infinite Democracy." In *Democracy in What State?* Ed. Giorgio Agamben et al.; trans. William McCuaig, pp. 58–75. New York: Columbia University Press, 2012.

National Public Radio. "Designing the Modern Office Space." *The Diane Rehm Show*, January 23, 2014. http://thedianerehmshow.org/shows/2014-01-23/designing-modern-office-space

"The Onrushing Wave." *The Economist* (The Future of Jobs), January 18, 2014, p. 24.

Orwell, George. *1984*. New York: Penguin, 1981.

Peristiany, J. G. "Law." In *The Institutions of Primitive Society: A Series of Broadcast Talks*, by E. E. Evans-Pritchard, Raymond

Firth, E. R. Leach, J. G. Peristiany, John Layard, Max Gluck-
man, Meyer Fortes, and Godfrey Lienhardt, pp. 39–49. Oxford,
UK: Blackwell, 1954.

Plato. *Republic*. Trans. G.M.A. Grube. Indianapolis, IN: Hackett,
1992.

Rancière, Jacques. "Democracies Against Democracy: An Interview with Eric Hazan." In *Democracy in What State?* Ed. Giorgio Agamben et al.; trans. William McCuaig, pp. 76–81. New
York: Columbia University Press, 2012.

Tocqueville, Alexis de. *Democracy in America*. New York: Harper
& Row, 1966.

Wolf, Eric. *Europe and the People Without History*. Berkeley: University of California Press, 1982.

Žižek, Slavoj. *Did Somebody Say Totalitarianism: Five Interventions
in the (Mis)use of a Notion*. London and New York: Verso, 2001.

———. "From Democracy to Divine Violence." In *Democracy in
What State?* Ed. Giorgio Agamben et al.; trans. William McCuaig,
pp. 100–120. New York: Columbia University Press, 2012.

———. "Have Michael Hardt and Antonio Negri Rewritten the
Communist Manifesto for the Twenty-First Century?" *Rethink-
ing Marxism*, no. 3/4 (2001). http://www.lacan.com/zizek-empire
.htm

———. *Welcome to the Desert of the Real*. London and New York:
Verso, 2002.

———. "Why We All Love to Hate Haider." *New Left Review* 2
(2000): 37–45.

CPSIA information can be obtained
at www.ICGtesting.com
Printed in the USA
LVOW12s0317290617
539750LV00001B/126/P